A Taste of
JULIE JORDAN

Andrew Shumaker

Now head chef at Omega Institute in Rhinebeck, New York, JULIE JORDAN was the original owner of the famous Cabbagetown Café in Ithaca, New York. She studied at the Cordon Bleu in London and is a frequent guest lecturer/chef at restaurants and retreat centers nationwide. She is the author of *Wings of Life* and the *Cabbagetown Café Cookbook*, both significant contributions to vegetarian cuisine. Julie's home is in Trumansburg, New York.

A Taste of
JULIE JORDAN

100 TOP VEGETARIAN CLASSICS

Julie Jordan

LARSON PUBLICATIONS
BURDETT, NY

International Standard Book Number: 0-943914-88-4
Library of Congress Catalog Card Number: 98-67553

Published for the Paul Brunton Philosophic Foundation by
Larson Publications
4936 NYS Route 414
Burdett, NY 14818 USA

Printed in Canada

06 05 04 03 02 01 00 99
10 9 8 7 6 5 4 3 2 1

Contents

Acknowledgments

My gratitude

To Varsha Dandakar and Craig Mack for major contributions to my repertoire of tastes and textures. To Stina Almroth, Steve Friedmutter, and Mindy Pushkin whose names have come to be known as part of their wonderful recipes.

To Elaine Gill for editing and publishing my first two cookbooks, and for pushing me to do this one.

To Karen Lehmann, Barbara Schramm, Carol Lee Fritz, Beth Bannister, and Barbara Nowogrodzki for helping me remain light and enthusiastic.

To the Omega Institute kitchen for showing me once again that people like to be creative cooks but they *really* like recipes.

To Amy Opperman Cash, June Fritchman, Kate Thomas, Flora Maranca, and all the friends and staff of Larson Publications who pulled this book together.

For everyone who has cooked with me

Introduction

I've always had two careers, one as a cook and the other as a writer. In many ways my cookbooks express who I am at the points when they're written. Not only do they reveal how I prepare food, how I think of food, and how I eat, but in a very essential way provide a map of how I live my life. *A Taste of Julie Jordan* is no exception. Although my original intention was to compile a collection of the best and most popular recipes from my earlier books, I found as the creative process began to work that I was embarking on another autobiographical journey.

So my cooking now comes from my studying macrobiotics and from my traveling around the United States. In Austin, Texas, I cooked the light flexible southern version of macrobiotic food. In Princeton, New Jersey, I learned the art of gourmet vegetarian deli food. In New Mexico I lived and breathed red and green chile, fresh pinto beans, posole. All this is part of who I am now and part of my offering to you.

I find that my cooking style now is much lighter, using less dairy or cutting out dairy altogether. I have reflected this in revising many of the recipes from *Cabbagetown Café Cookbook* and *Wings of Life*. There are dozens of new recipes and almost two hundred variations and options.

Since it seems that everyone has their own version of what "vegetarian" means, I should say that by *vegetarian* in this book I mean ovo-lacto vegetarian; this includes eggs, dairy products, and honey, but not meat, fish, or animal seafood. By *vegan* I mean recipes with no animal products whatsoever, not even honey. My publishers have chosen to identify recipes that are either vegan or have a vegan option with a ◍. Sometimes the difference is as simple as using olive oil instead of butter.

The new recipes like Salsa Fresca, Pad Thai, Vietnamese Pasta Salad, Toasted-Corn Polenta, and New Mexico Red Chile Enchiladas resonate with the "going into the next century" palate. Many of them are loaded with lively, trendy ingredients like fresh cilantro, esoteric chile peppers, rice noodles, peanut sauce, and more.

To me, the freshness of the food and grain is essential. Equally so is a fresh and lively attitude in the person preparing the food. Finally, it is important to go through your kitchen and clean it out. I call this "eliminating stagnation." Throw out the old spices and dusty pasta; have a yard sale and sell all the pots and pans and dishes you never use; scrub all the shelves. A kitchen should be clean, functional, and streamlined.

Cooking is a wonderful creative adventure and I hope you all enjoy it!

What to Feed Hungry People While You Cook

I enjoy having my friends and guests standing around talking with me while I cook. While they wait for dinner, I put a nice bottle of wine and a few appetizers on the counter or table for them. This lingering first course is often the most fun part of the meal.

If you are having a substantial meal, go with a light appetizer such as Marinated Mushrooms and baguettes with Fresh Herb Butter—or perhaps a big basket of warm Garlic Bread. A spicy Mexican meal can be started off with Salsa Fresca, Guacamole, and Refried Beans and tortilla chips. If you are going Indian, I recommend the Onion, Cabbage, Spinach, or Zucchini Pakoras. Sourdough bread is always great served with spreads such as Hummus, Guacamole, or the Nut & Mushroom Pâté. Or, your creative side may want to arrange a big relish tray of fresh and blanched vegetables, Marinated Brussels Sprouts, Herbed Baked Tofu, an assortment of olives, and one or more of the dips or salad dressings.

At the very least, have a bowl of fresh Tamari-Roasted Almonds that your guests won't be able to stop eating.

Bon appetit!

Refried Beans

The hearty spicy refries from Cabbagetown Café have pleased people for many years. Serve as a dip for tortilla chips, on nachos, with enchiladas, on tostados.

2 cups uncooked pinto or black beans

6 cups water

½ stick kombu seaweed

2 bay leaves

1 tablespoon ground cumin

1 teaspoon ground coriander

½ teaspoon cayenne

½ teaspoon black pepper

½ teaspoon dried or finely chopped fresh oregano

½ teaspoon dried basil or 2 teaspoons finely chopped fresh basil

½ teaspoon dried dill weed or 1 tablespoon finely chopped fresh dill

½ cup finely chopped cilantro

2½ teaspoons salt

3 tablespoons light vegetable oil

1 onion, chopped

1 green pepper, chopped

4 cloves of garlic, finely chopped

1 tablespoon olive oil (optional: to reheat beans)

1. Sort the beans carefully for stones, rinse, and soak overnight. Pour off soaking water. Put the beans with 6 cups of water, kombu seaweed, and bay leaves in a medium-size pot. Bring to a boil for 10 minutes, skimming off the foam. Reduce the heat and simmer, partially covered, stirring occasionally to keep the beans from sticking. Cook for about 2 hours, or until the beans are very soft.

2. Measure out the spices, herbs, and salt and mix them together so they are ready to use.

3. In a frying pan, heat the 3 tablespoons oil. Add the onion, green pepper, and garlic and saute for about 3 minutes, until limp. Reduce the heat, add the spice and salt mixture, and saute for 2 minutes more, stirring frequently so nothing sticks and burns.

4. Remove the bay leaves and mash the cooked beans until smooth. Use a potato masher or bean masher or any other mashing device you have. Mash in the vegetable-spice mixture.

5. Continue to cook over very low heat for 15–20 minutes to blend the flavors. Stir often.

6. These beans can be served immediately as is without any further cooking. To reheat the beans, heat 1 tablespoon olive oil in a pan. Add the beans and fry, stirring frequently, until the beans are hot. Taste and reseason.

YIELD: 6 CUPS

Tamari-Roasted Almonds

Heap up a bowl! These flavorful almonds are good for nibbling and excellent in salads.

1½ cups almonds

2 tablespoons tamari or soy sauce

1. Toast the almonds in a 350° oven or toaster oven for about 25 minutes, or until lightly browned.

2. Mix in the tamari or soy sauce.

3. Return to the oven for 5 minutes so the tamari can bake into the almonds. Do not bake any longer or the tamari will burn.

4. Use the roasted almonds whole or chop them in half.

5. These are best if served immediately, but they will stay crisp stored in a covered jar at room temperature for about a week.

YIELD: 1½ CUPS

Salsa Fresca

This is a wonderful fresh salsa to eat with tortilla chips or put on top of burritos. It is particularly good in the summer when you can use tomatoes, cilantro, and hot peppers fresh from the garden.

4 cloves of garlic, finely chopped

Juice of 1 lemon or 1 lime

1 red or white onion, finely chopped

1 jalapeno or other fresh hot pepper(s), finely chopped, or 1 teaspoon dried red pepper flakes

3 large fresh tomatoes, or 6 small fresh tomatoes, or 2 cups canned tomatoes, finely chopped

1 tablespoon olive oil

1 teaspoon sea salt

Freshly ground black pepper to taste

2 tablespoons finely chopped fresh cilantro

1. Marinate the garlic in lemon or lime juice for 10–15 minutes.

2. Add all other ingredients and mix together. Let sit for 1 hour so everything marinates.

3. Taste and adjust seasonings.

4. If you keep this salsa for a second day, cook it for about 20 minutes to give it a new life.

Salsa with Roasted Hot Peppers

Roast the hot peppers in a flame till they collapse. Put them in a paper bag for a few minutes to steam the skins loose, then peel, chop finely and add to the salsa in step 2. This gives the salsa a good smoky flavor.

Salsa with Chopped Black Olives or Chopped Ripe Avocado

Add these ingredients to the salsa in step 2.

YIELD: 3 CUPS

4 Guacamole

I learned to make guacamole this way in New Mexico. Sweet white onions are the best. Hass avocados are by far the richest and best-flavored variety.

2 cloves garlic

¼ cup finely chopped sweet white onion

Juice of 1 lemon or 1 lime

1 ripe avocado (You want it to respond to firm pressure from your thumb.)

Salt to taste

1–2 tablespoons chopped cilantro

1. Marinate the garlic and onion in lemon or lime juice for 10–15 minutes.

2. Add the avocado and cut in with a pastry blender or 2 forks until texture is medium-smooth.

3. Mix in salt and cilantro to taste.

4. Serve immediately with tortilla chips.

Creamy Guacamole

Mix in 1–2 tablespoons sour cream in step 3. (This variation is not vegan.)

YIELD: ABOUT I CUP.

SERVES 2

5The World's Best Garlic Bread

Sixteen cloves seem like a lot of garlic, but the garlic blends with the butter and tomatoes to give you a rich and soul-warming taste. Serve this garlic bread with the first course, or with a big salad, or with pasta.

1 cup butter, at room temperature

16 cloves (2 bulbs) of garlic, finely chopped

¼ cup finely chopped fresh parsley

½ cup freshly grated parmesan cheese

1 teaspoon dried or finely chopped fresh oregano

¼ teaspoon salt

1 cup drained canned tomatoes or 2 fresh tomatoes,
    chopped into small pieces

8–12 slices whole wheat bread (Homemade bread is best.)

1. In a medium-size mixing bowl, beat the softened butter until it's smooth.

2. Mix in the garlic, parsley, parmesan cheese, oregano, and salt.

3. Mix in the tomatoes, but don't mix until they are smooth. You want the tomatoes to stay in irregular lumps.

4. Spread the mixture thickly on the slices of bread.

5. Lay out flat on baking trays and bake in a preheated 350° oven for about 25–30 minutes, until the butter is melted in and the slices look hot and delicious.

YIELD: SERVES 8–12

Onion Pakoras

These spicy fritters from India always steal the show.

> 6 onions, cut in crescents
>
> Juice of 2 lemons
>
> 1 tablespoon salt (Yes, I mean a *tablespoon*.)
>
> 1 teaspoon cayenne
>
> 1 tablespoon ground cumin
>
> 1 tablespoon cumin seeds
>
> 2 cups chick pea flour
>
> Light vegetable oil for frying

1. Mix together the onions, lemon juice, salt, and spices. In India the mixing is done vigorously with the hands. Squeeze the spices into the onions. Let sit for 30–60 minutes. The onions will throw off juice, which will be part of the batter with the chick pea flour later.

2. After the sitting time, mix in the chick pea flour.

3. In a medium-size frying pan, measure oil about ½ inch deep and heat until a tiny bit of the batter dropped in it sizzles. Pull out small handfuls of the onion mixture and drop them in the oil. Fry each pakora until browned and crisp, turning once. Drain on paper towels or on a brown paper bag.

4. Serve hot. These are best absolutely fresh, but they heat up nicely in the oven.

Crisp Onion Pakoras

Add 2–3 tablespoons rice flour to make a crisper pakora.

Cabbage or Spinach Pakoras

Replace 2 of the onions with 2 cups very finely cut cabbage or spinach.

Zucchini Pakoras

Replace 2 of the onions with 2 cups grated zucchini.

YIELD: 32 PAKORAS.

SERVES 8–12

Hummus

Hummus is the delicious, deeply nourishing staple of vegetarian cuisine. This particular recipe is one people swear by. Serve as a dip with carrot, celery, and cucumber sticks, radishes, whole scallions, or steamed broccoli. Serve as a spread on crackers. Or serve with baguettes, or in pita bread with sprouts and chopped red onion, sliced tomatoes, or cucumbers.

> 1 cup uncooked chick peas or 2 cups cooked or canned chick peas
>
> 5 cups water
>
> ½ stick kombu seaweed
>
> 2 bay leaves
>
> 2 cloves of garlic, finely chopped
>
> ½ teaspoon salt
>
> ¾ cup tahini
>
> Juice of 1 lemon
>
> About ¼ cup chick pea cooking liquid or water
>
> ½ cup finely chopped fresh parsley
>
> 2 tablespoons finely chopped fresh chives or scallions
>
> 1 celery stalk, finely chopped (optional)

1. Sort the chick peas for stones, rinse, and soak overnight. Pour off the soaking water. Put the chick peas, water, kombu, and bay leaves in a medium-size pot. Bring to a boil for 10 minutes, skimming off the foam. Reduce the heat and simmer, partially covered, stirring occasionally to keep the chick peas from sticking. Cook for 2–3 hours, or until the chick peas are very tender.

2. In a medium-size bowl, mix the garlic, salt, and tahini with a wooden spoon. Mix in the lemon juice a little at a time, alternating with the chick pea cooking liquid. Continue adding liquid until the mixture whips up and lightens in color. Even if the mixture appears to curdle, just keep adding liquid and beating. It will come together. Getting the whipped consistency is crucial for the final consistency of the hummus.

3. Grind the chick peas through a meat grinder, grain mill, or food processor. A blender will not work.

4. Stir the chick peas into the tahini mixture. Add the parsley, chives or scallions, and celery. If the mixture is too thick, stir in more chick pea liquid until it's fluffy.

5. Taste. You might want to add more salt, lemon juice, or parsley.

YIELD: 3 CUPS

Marinated Brussels Sprouts

These are so good you won't believe it. Serve with sourdough bread and your favorite spread.

1 pound brussels sprouts

1 cup Tarragon Vinaigrette Dressing (page 46)

1 teaspoon fennel seeds

1. Prepare the brussels sprouts by rinsing them and trimming off the browned tips of the stems and any yellowed leaves. Cut an X in the bottom stem end of each sprout so they'll cook evenly. Steam or blanch for 8–12 minutes, until they are barely tender when pierced with a fork. Pour through a colander to drain off the water.

2. Prepare the dressing. Mix the fennel seeds into the dressing. Pour into a medium-size pot and simmer for 1–2 minutes to blend the flavors. Add the cooked sprouts and toss together. Remove from the heat and allow to cool, tossing occasionally so all the sprouts are covered with dressing.

3. Serve at room temperature. You can store them in the refrigerator and remove 30 minutes before serving so they can warm up.

Marinated Mushrooms

Rinse 1 pound of mushrooms thoroughly and trim off any browned spots. Drop the mushrooms into a pot of boiling water and boil for 5 minutes. Pour through a colander to drain the water. Then proceed as with brussels sprouts in steps 2 and 3.

YIELD: SERVES 4–6

Nut & Mushroom Pâté

Delicious! I use this for receptions, weddings, and picnics. Luckily for me many of my friends have adopted it too, so I'm served Nut & Mushroom Pâté as an appetizer when I go to their houses for dinner. Serve as a spread for baguettes or as a dip for carrot sticks.

½ cup mixed nuts and seeds (I recommend almonds, sunflower seeds, and walnuts. Sesame seeds don't give a good texture.)

2 tablespoons olive oil

1 onion, finely chopped

1 pound mushrooms, very finely chopped

½ cup crumbled tofu

¼ cup olive oil

¼ cup tahini

2 tablespoons tamari or soy sauce

Juice of ½ lemon

1 clove of garlic, finely chopped

½ teaspoon dried or finely chopped fresh oregano

½ teaspoon dried or finely chopped fresh tarragon

½ teaspoon mustard powder

Salt to taste

1. Toast the nuts and seeds in a toaster oven or in a frying pan until lightly browned.

2. Heat 2 tablespoons oil in a frying pan and add the onion and mushrooms. Fry until the mixture is dark brown and dry. Do not burn.

3. In a blender, combine the tofu, ¼ cup oil, the tahini, tamari, lemon juice, and seasonings and blend until smooth. Add the toasted nuts and seeds, and blend until almost smooth. (A little crunchy texture is nice here.)

4. Remove the blended mixture to a bowl. Stir in the mushrooms and onion.

5. Allow to cool, then taste for salt.

YIELD: 2 CUPS

Fresh Herb Butter

This spread is delicious and lighter than butter. It's fun to use different herbs, fresh from the garden. Serve herb butter with baguettes or sourdough bread.

2 cloves garlic

Juice of ½ lemon

¼ pound butter

¼ cup olive oil

¼ cup finely chopped fresh green herbs (Chives, dill, parsley, chervil, small amounts of basil, thyme, oregano, and mint are all good.)

¼ teaspoon salt

1. Chop the garlic up fine and marinate for 10–15 minutes in the lemon juice.

2. Cream the butter until smooth (by hand or in the food processor). Beat in olive oil, herbs, salt, and garlic-lemon mixture.

3. Taste and correct the seasonings.

4. Serve in a bowl alongside an uncut crusty loaf of bread and bread knife on a cutting board.

YIELD: ¼–¾ CUP.

ENOUGH FOR I BAGUETTE OR SOURDOUGH LOAF

Soups

The soup recipes here are hearty,
nutritious, and delicious. All are tried and true.

The bean and grain soups warm any cold winter day or night.
The lighter soups, such as Carrot Ginger Soup or Corn
Chowder, and the cold soups can also be a wonderful balance to
a hot summer day.

Soup with bread can be a meal in itself. Or, add a salad
for "Soup, Salad, and Bread." Simple soups, such as Miso Soup
or the Cream of Butternut Squash Soup, can accompany
cooked grains at a meal.

For never-fail "American-style" fare, I suggest Split Pea Barley,
Spinach Lentil, or the Hearty Vegetable soups. Many of the
soups can be combined with other recipes in this book for
a wonderful ethnic meal. The Black Bean Soup, for example,
is traditionally Caribbean or Mexican. Indian soups are usually
served as part of the meal—try Indian Lentil Soup,
Cabbage Dal, or Indian Spinach & Peanut Soup.

Black Bean Soup

What really makes this recipe special is the addition of green olives.

2 cups uncooked black beans

8 cups water

2 bay leaves

¼ cup olive oil

2 onions, finely chopped

2 green peppers, finely chopped

4 cloves of garlic, finely chopped

1 tablespoon cumin

1 teaspoon dried or finely chopped fresh oregano

1 teaspoon mustard powder

1 teaspoon dried dill weed or 1 tablespoon finely chopped fresh dill

½ cup chopped green olives, drained

1 teaspoon salt

Juice of 1 lemon

Sour cream (*optional, non-vegan*)

1. Sort the beans for stones, rinse, and soak overnight. Pour off the soaking water. Put the black beans, water, and bay leaves in a soup pot. Bring to a boil, then reduce the heat and simmer, partially covered, stirring occasionally to keep the beans from sticking. Cook for about 2 hours, or until the beans are soft.

2. In a separate frying pan, heat the olive oil. Add the onions, green peppers, and garlic and saute until limp and lightly browned. Add the spices and herbs. Saute for a few minutes, adding more oil if necessary to keep from sticking. Add the olives and cook 5 minutes.

3. Using a potato masher or a bean masher or a fork, mash about ¼ of the beans into a paste to give the soup a good thick texture. You can do this in the soup pot or remove the beans, mash them, and return.

4. Add the cooked vegetables to the beans, along with the salt and the lemon juice. Continue simmering for as long as possible.

5. Taste and adjust the seasonings. You might want to add more salt.

6. Serve plain or top each bowl with a dollop of sour cream.

YIELD: SERVES 6

Miso Soup

Different misos are like fine wines—rich, with a wide variety of flavors. A dark barley or brown rice miso makes a hearty soup. A lighter sweet brown rice, sweet white, or chick pea miso makes a light summer soup. I have found that some American misos are much less salty than Japanese miso, so if using American miso use the amount of miso in the recipe, then add a bit more if needed, and add a pinch or two of salt or a small amount of tamari to taste. Choose one to three vegetables for each soup. I especially like carrots, daikon, onions, cabbage, turnips, rutabagas, green beans, and yellow summer squash.

> **4 cups water**
> **½-inch piece wakame seaweed**
> **2 cups chopped vegetables**
> **2–3 tablespoons miso**
> **½ cup cold water**
> **Juice from 1 tablespoon grated ginger (optional)**
> **Finely chopped parsley or scallions**
> **Tamari or sea salt to taste**

1. Measure the water into your soup pot. Start heating it.

2. Using scissors, snip the wakame seaweed into tiny pieces into the soup.

3. Cut the vegetables you've chosen uniformly, whether in thin slices, chunks, or diced. It is important all the vegetable pieces be the same size so they cook at the same speed.

4. When the water boils add the vegetables. Cook until the vegetables are just done, tender but not soft.

5. Dissolve the miso in ½ cup cold water in a separate cup or bowl. The exact amount of miso you'll need depends on how richly flavored your miso is and how you like your soup. With a miso with which you have no prior experience start with the smaller amount, then add more to taste. Miso soup that tastes strong or thick has too much miso. Soup that tastes watery has too little miso.

6. Add the miso liquid to the hot soup. This is the only tricky step with miso soup. Miso is a live culture. You want to cook the miso just enough to activate it, but you don't want to boil it or you'll kill the culture. The miso is activated when the soup broth changes from clear to cloudy. This takes about 10 seconds. Turn off the heat immediately. If using ginger juice, add it now.

7. Add tamari or salt to taste.

8. Serve each bowl garnished with parsley or scallions. (This is the green of life floating in the sea.)

Richer Miso Soup

Very lightly saute the vegetables in 1 tablespoon toasted sesame oil before adding to the soup. This will bring out the vegetables' flavor.

YIELD: SERVES 4

Split Pea Barley Soup

This savory soup is very simple to make. It's my favorite soup, a staple of my wintertime existence.

2 cups uncooked green split peas

⅓ cup uncooked barley

10 cups water

2 bay leaves

2 tablespoons light olive oil

1 onion, finely chopped

1 carrot, finely chopped

2 cloves of garlic, finely chopped

1 teaspoon dried or finely chopped fresh thyme

1 teaspoon salt

1. Sort the split peas for stones. Measure the split peas, barley, water, and bay leaves into a soup pot. Bring to a boil, then reduce the heat and simmer, partially covered, stirring occasionally to keep the peas from sticking. Cook for about 45 minutes, or until the peas and barley are tender.

2. Heat the oil in a separate frying pan. Add the onion, carrot, garlic, and thyme, and saute until the carrot pieces are tender.

3. Add the cooked vegetables to the split peas, along with the salt. Continue simmering for at least 30 minutes to blend the flavors, stirring frequently.

4. Taste and adjust the seasonings. Sometimes black pepper tastes good.

YIELD: SERVES 6

Spinach Lentil Soup

This soup, more than any other of my published soups, has been adopted by restaurants. Many times in my travels, I've been delighted to taste my personal blend of lentils, potatoes, and dill.

1 cup uncooked brown lentils

⅓ cup uncooked green split peas

7 cups water

2 bay leaves

2 potatoes

2 tablespoons olive oil

2 onions, finely chopped

2 cloves of garlic, finely chopped

1 tablespoon dried dill weed or 2 tablespoons finely chopped fresh dill

½ teaspoon black pepper

8–10 ounces fresh spinach, swiss chard, or kale, finely chopped (6 cups)

1 teaspoon salt

2 tablespoons red wine vinegar or lemon juice

1. Sort the lentils and green split peas for stones. Measure the lentils, split peas, water, and bay leaves into a soup pot. Bring to a boil, then reduce the heat and simmer, partially covered, stirring occasionally to keep the lentils and peas from sticking. Cook for about 30 minutes, or until the lentils are tender.

2. Scrub the potatoes well but do not peel. Dice in small cubes and cook in water to cover until the cubes are cooked but still firm, about 5 minutes after the water boils.

3. In a separate frying pan, heat the olive oil. Add the onions and saute for a minute or two; then add the garlic, dill, and pepper. Saute a few minutes more. Add part of the spinach, chard, or kale. Wait for it to wilt, then add more. Continue until all the spinach, chard, or kale is in the pan and lightly cooked.

4. Add the potatoes, potato water, spinach mixture, and salt to the lentils. Continue to simmer for at least 30 minutes to blend the flavors, stirring frequently.

5. About 10 minutes before serving, mix in the vinegar or lemon juice. A dash of vinegar or lemon juice enhances the flavor of many bean soups. Cook 10 minutes more, then taste and adjust the seasonings.

YIELD: SERVES 6

15 Cream of Butternut Squash Soup

This soup is a dream for mellow autumn days. I like serving it with thin slices of sourdough bread, pan-fried in olive oil until light brown.

1 butternut or kabocha squash (about 2 pounds)

2 tablespoons olive oil

2 medium onions, cut in chunks

1 teaspoon salt

3 cups water

Freshly ground black pepper

2 green onions or scallions with tender green tops, chopped

1. Cut the squash into chunks. All commercial squash needs to be peeled because the skins are waxed. Homegrown or organic squash such as butternut or kabocha with soft skins don't need to be peeled and their skins soften entirely during cooking.

2. Pour the olive oil into a large soup pot. Add squash and onions. Add the salt. Cover and cook over medium heat, stirring occasionally, about 20 minutes. Watch closely so the vegetables don't dry out and burn. This initial cooking in oil develops the rich sweet flavors of the vegetables.

3. Add the 3 cups water. Continue cooking until the vegetables are very soft, about 20 minutes. Puree in a blender or food processor until smooth. Add a bit more water if the soup is too thick, but be careful since too much water knocks out the lovely rich flavor.

4. Taste and correct seasonings. If you have a good squash, you shouldn't need to do anything more, except perhaps add a pinch of salt. Heat the soup to the temperature you want (but not to boiling).

5. Top each serving with freshly ground black pepper and chopped green onions.

YIELD: SERVES 4

Cabbage Dal

This Indian soup is thick and very flavorful.

1 cup uncooked red lentils

3 cups water

2 bay leaves

¼ cup light vegetable oil

2 teaspoons black mustard seeds

¼ teaspoon asafetida

1 fresh hot pepper, finely chopped

4 cloves of garlic, finely chopped

½-inch piece fresh ginger, finely chopped

1 teaspoon turmeric

2 onions, chopped

1 big wedge green cabbage, finely chopped (4 cups)

1 quart canned tomatoes

2 teaspoons salt

1 teaspoon molasses

5 teaspoons ground cumin

4 teaspoons ground coriander

¼ teaspoon cayenne

Juice of 1 lemon

1. Sort the lentils carefully for stones and rinse. Measure the lentils, water, and bay leaves into a medium-size pot. Bring to a boil, then reduce the heat and simmer, partially covered, stirring occasionally to keep the lentils from sticking. Cook for about 20 minutes, or until the lentils are soft.

2. In a soup pot, heat the oil. When you drop a mustard seed in the hot oil and it sizzles, the temperature is right. Pour in the mustard seeds and cook until they pop. Lower the heat and stir frequently so you don't burn any of the seeds. Stir in the asafetida, then the chopped hot pepper, then the garlic and ginger, then the turmeric. Cook for 3–4 minutes, stirring frequently.

3. Add the onions. Stir and cook for 10 minutes. Add the cabbage. Cook for 15 minutes.

4. Crush the canned tomatoes with your hands or the back of a spoon to get small pieces. Add to the soup, along with the accompanying tomato juice, the salt, and the molasses. Cook for 20 minutes, or until hot. Stir frequently so nothing sticks.

5. Stir in the ground cumin, coriander, and cayenne. Add the cooked lentils and water. Continue simmering for at least 30 minutes to blend the flavors. Add the lemon juice.

6. Taste and adjust the seasonings.

YIELD: SERVES 6

Carrot Ginger Soup

Good sweet organic carrots make the best soup! This soup is good served hot, at room temperature, or cold.

2 onions, chopped

1 pound carrots, cut into chunks (about 2 ½ cups)

6 cups water

3 tablespoons light miso

½ cup cold water

Juice from 2 tablespoons grated ginger

Salt to taste

1. Cook the onions and carrots in water until tender.

2. Blend in a food processor until smooth. Return to cooking pot.

3. In a small cup or bowl, dissolve the miso in cold water. Add to the soup. Bring the soup just up to a boil and turn off the heat.

4. Squeeze in ginger juice.

5. Salt to taste. The flavor should be simple, fresh, and balanced—one pure tone.

YIELD: SERVES 4

Indian Lentil Soup

This soup has that genuine Indian taste you don't often find in American versions of Indian food—rich, well rounded, soul filling spiciness.

1 ½ cups uncooked brown lentils

4 cups water

2 bay leaves

¼ cup light vegetable oil

2 tablespoons black mustard seeds

2 tablespoons cumin seeds

¼ teaspoon asafetida

1 fresh hot pepper, finely chopped

4 cloves of garlic, finely chopped

½-inch piece fresh ginger, finely chopped

1 teaspoon turmeric

2 onions, chopped

½ cup dried unsweetened or grated fresh coconut

1 tablespoon light vegetable oil

1 quart canned tomatoes

2 teaspoons salt

2 tablespoons ground cumin

2 tablespoons ground coriander

¼ teaspoon cayenne

1. Sort the lentils for stones and rinse. Measure the lentils, water, and bay leaves into a medium-size pot. Bring to a boil then reduce the heat and simmer, partially covered, stirring occasionally to keep the lentils from sticking. Cook for about 30 minutes or until the lentils are tender.

2. In a soup pot, heat the oil. When you drop a mustard seed in the hot oil and it sizzles, the temperature is right. Pour in the mustard seeds and cumin seeds, and cook until most of them pop. Lower the heat and stir frequently so you don't burn any of the seeds. Stir in the asafetida, then the chopped hot pepper, the garlic and ginger, then the turmeric. Cook for 3–4 minutes, stirring frequently.

3. Add the onions. Stir and cook for 10 minutes. Add the coconut along with 1 tablespoon oil, then cook for 10 minutes more.

4. Crush the canned tomatoes with your hand or the back of a spoon to get small pieces. Add to the soup, along with the accompanying tomato juice and the salt. Cook for 20 minutes or until hot. Stir frequently so nothing sticks.

5. Stir in the ground cumin, coriander, and cayenne. Add the cooked lentils and water. Continue to simmer for at least 30 minutes. Taste and reseason.

YIELD: SERVES 6

Indian Spinach & Peanut Soup

This unique Indian soup is well worth the work it takes to make it.

2 potatoes
8–10 ounces fresh spinach or swiss chard, chopped (6 cups)
4 cups water
2 cups peanuts, raw or roasted
¼ cup light vegetable oil
4 teaspoons cumin seeds
4 cloves of garlic, finely chopped
1 fresh hot pepper, finely chopped
¼ teaspoon asafetida
1 teaspoon turmeric
2 teaspoons salt
1 teaspoon ground cumin
1 teaspoon ground coriander
¼ teaspoon cayenne
½ cup sour cream
½ cup yoghurt

1. Scrub the potatoes well but do not peel. Dice in small cubes. Put in a large pot. Put the chopped spinach on top and pour in the water. Bring the water to a boil, then reduce the heat and simmer, covered, for about 10 minutes, or until the potatoes are cooked.

continues . . .

2. Meanwhile, make the peanuts into roasted peanut meal. If you are starting with raw peanuts, roast them in a dry skillet for about 10 minutes, or until dark spots appear. Stir frequently so the peanuts don't burn. Allow to cool. Grind them in a grain mill, or at low speed in a blender or food processor. Don't grind too fast or you will make peanut butter. If you are starting with roasted peanuts, grind them as above.

3. In a soup pot, heat the oil. Add the cumin seeds and garlic. When the garlic is cooked to a light brown color, add the hot pepper, then the asafetida, then the turmeric. Cook for 3–4 minutes.

4. Add the cooked potatoes, spinach, and water. Stir well. Then add the salt, ground cumin, coriander, and cayenne.

5. Add the peanut meal. Cook for 15 minutes to blend the flavors.

6. Remove a little hot soup from the pot and stir the yoghurt and sour cream into it. Return it to the rest of the soup. Simmer for 15 minutes, stirring frequently.

YIELD: SERVES 6

Thick Tomato Soup with Green Peas & Marjoram

This quick never-fail soup is thick with vegetables. You can leave it vegetably or make it into a bisque smooth with sour cream.

1 quart tomato juice

1 carrot, finely grated

3 celery stalks, finely chopped

4 scallions, finely chopped

2 tablespoons olive oil

1 onion, finely chopped

1 green pepper, finely chopped

2 cloves of garlic, finely chopped

1 teaspoon dried basil or 1 tablespoon finely chopped fresh basil

½ teaspoon dried marjoram or 2 teaspoons finely chopped fresh marjoram

¼–½ teaspoon black pepper

1 medium-size zucchini, finely chopped, or 8–10 ounces fresh spinach
(finely chopped)

1 cup green peas, fresh or frozen

1. In a soup pot, bring the tomato juice to a boil, then add the carrot, celery, and scallions. Reduce the heat and continue to simmer.

2. In a separate frying pan, heat the oil. Add the onion, green pepper, and garlic and saute until limp. Add the herbs and pepper and saute for about 1 minute. Add the zucchini or spinach and green peas and cook until tender.

3. Add the cooked vegetables to the tomato mixture. Simmer for 30 minutes.

4. Salt the soup to taste.

Tomato Bisque

Just before serving, remove 1–2 cups of the soup to a separate bowl. Mix thoroughly with 1 cup sour cream, then return to the rest of the soup, and stir thoroughly. (This variation is non-vegan.)

YIELD: SERVES 6

Corn Chowder

This is a gift from "Aunt Hooniata," Cabbagetown's best chowder cook.

3 potatoes
3 tablespoons butter
1 onion, finely diced
2 cloves of garlic, finely chopped
1 carrot, finely diced
3 celery stalks, finely diced
3 cups fresh or frozen corn
½ teaspoon dried marjoram or 2 teaspoons finely chopped fresh marjoram
H teaspoon dried or finely chopped fresh thyme
¼ teaspoon paprika
¼ teaspoon black pepper
1 teaspoon salt
2–3 cups milk
Chives or parsley for garnish (optional)

1. Scrub the potatoes well but do not peel. Cook in water to cover until the potatoes are cooked but still firm, about 30 minutes after the water boils.

2. In a soup pot, melt the butter. Add the onion, garlic, carrot, and celery and saute until the vegetables are cooked but not too soft. Add the corn and cook for 10 minutes more. Add the herbs, spices, and salt and cook for 3–4 minutes more.

3. Dice 1 ½ potatoes into small cubes. Add to the soup pot.

4. Blend the remaining 1 ½ potatoes with the potato water and 2–3 cups milk, enough to make a good serving consistency.

5. Add the blended mixture to the soup pot. Heat gently to a serving temperature.

6. Taste and adjust the seasonings. Garnish with finely chopped chives or parsley if desired.

YIELD: SERVES 6

Mushroom Barley Soup

This is a classic soup that can be used with any kind of mushrooms.

½ cup uncooked barley

8 cups water

2 bay leaves

2 tablespoons olive oil

12 ounces mushrooms (any type), sliced

1 carrot, thinly sliced

2 celery stalks, thinly sliced

1 cup fresh or frozen lima beans (optional)

½ teaspoon dried or finely chopped fresh thyme

½ teaspoon black pepper

¼ cup tamari or soy sauce

¼ cup finely chopped fresh chives or scallions

¼ cup finely chopped fresh parsley

1. Measure the barley, water, and bay leaves into a soup pot. Bring to a boil, then reduce the heat and simmer, partially covered, stirring occasionally to keep the barley from sticking. Cook for about 1 hour, or until the barley is tender.

2. In a separate frying pan, heat the oil. Add the mushrooms and saute over high heat, searing them to get maximum flavor. Lower the heat and add the carrot, celery, and lima beans. Cook for 10–15 minutes, or until the vegetables are tender. Add the thyme and pepper, and cook for 2–3 minutes more.

3. Add the cooked vegetables to the soup pot, along with the tamari, chives or scallions, and parsley.

4. Continue to simmer for 30 minutes to blend the flavors. Taste and adjust the seasonings. This soup gets very thick. When you reheat it, add more water, then reseason it with tamari, pepper, and more chopped parsley to freshen it.

YIELD: SERVES 6

Hearty Vegetable Soup

This soup is featured on the front cover of this book when newly made. The first day it is full of wonderful tomato and fresh, vegetable flavors. The next day it takes on a much beanier flavor and is more like a bean stew. Both versions are good but very different.

¼ cup uncooked kidney beans

¼ cup uncooked pinto beans

¼ cup uncooked white pea beans

¼ uncooked black-eyed beans (You may use dried beans in any combination you choose as long as you have a total of 1 cup uncooked beans.)

12 cups water

2 bay leaves

¼ cup olive oil

2 large onions, chopped (3 cups)

5 cloves garlic, finely chopped

2 green peppers, cut into chunks

2 carrots, diced (optional)

1 teaspoon dried or finely chopped fresh oregano

2 teaspoons dried or 2 tablespoons finely chopped basil

2–3 teaspoons salt

½ teaspoon freshly ground pepper

1 large celery stalk, chopped

½ cup green beans, cut into approximately 1-inch pieces, fresh or frozen (optional)

2 quarts canned tomatoes

¼ cup finely chopped parsley

1 large fresh tomato or 6 cherry tomatoes, halved

¾ cup snap peas, fresh or frozen

½ cup green peas, fresh or frozen

Freshly grated parmesan cheese (*optional, non-vegan*)

1. Sort the beans for stones, rinse, and soak overnight. Pour off the soaking water. Combine the soaked beans, water, and bay leaves in a large soup pot. Bring to a boil, then reduce the heat and simmer, partially covered, for about 2–3 hours, or until the beans are tender.

2. In another large soup pot, heat the olive oil. Add onions and garlic and saute until onions are clear. Add the green peppers and carrots. Saute for 5 minutes more. Reduce heat and add the herbs, salt, and pepper, sauteeing for an additional 5 minutes, stirring frequently to keep it from sticking.

3. Add celery and green beans stirring all the time.

4. Crush the canned tomatoes with your hand or the back of a spoon to get small pieces. Add the tomatoes and juice to the vegetables and simmer for 15 minutes.

5. When the beans are tender, add them to the soup pot along with half of the bean cooking water. Add additional bean liquid or water to get the ideal consistency. Continue to simmer for 30–60 minutes to blend the flavors.

6. Add the fresh tomato, snap peas, green peas, and parsley. Taste and reseason as needed.

7. Serve as is or sprinkle each bowl with grated parmesan cheese if desired.

YIELD: SERVES 12

Cold Gazpacho

Here you have the number 1 cold soup, the summertime favorite at Cabbagetown. The recipe can be made with fresh or canned tomatoes, chopped by hand or in a blender or food processor. But, here are our ratings of gazpacho:

★★★★ *Best! hand-chopped with fresh tomatoes.*

★★★ *Hand-chopped, with canned tomatoes.*

★★ *Blended with fresh tomatoes.*

★ *Blended with canned tomatoes.*

Juice of 1 lemon or 1 lime

2 cloves of garlic, finely chopped

1 onion

1 cucumber, peeled

1 green pepper

6–8 fresh ripe tomatoes or 1 quart canned tomatoes

1 tablespoon good olive oil (The better the oil, the better the soup; if you don't have a good oil, leave it out.)

½ teaspoon salt

¼ teaspoon black pepper

1. Marinate the garlic in the lemon or lime juice for 10–15 minutes.

2. Chop all the vegetables as finely as your patience allows. Or combine all the vegetables, coarsely chopped, in a blender or food processor. Blend for a short time, then continue pulsing the machine on and off to get a nice, evenly chunked soup.

3. Mix in the olive oil, salt, pepper, and garlic and lemon or lime juice.

4. Chill thoroughly. Taste.

The Gazpacho Bar

Start with a big bowl of finely chopped tomatoes, chilled. Surround it with bowls of the other gazpacho vegetables, and bowls of chopped black olives, chopped hard-boiled eggs (non-vegan), chopped radishes, chopped scallions. Let each person assemble his or her own soup. Serve with crusty bread and your favorite spread.

YIELD: SERVES 6

Cold Borscht

This is the classic bright purple beet soup.

1 pound beets

2 bay leaves

2 tablespoons butter, OR olive oil (*vegan option*)

2 onions, chopped

1 carrot, chopped

1 wedge cabbage, chopped (4 cups)

Beet greens, chopped (optional)

2 teaspoons caraway seeds

1 teaspoon dried dill weed or 1 tablespoon finely chopped fresh dill

Juice of 2 lemons

½ teaspoon salt

¼ teaspoon black pepper

Sour cream (*optional, non-vegan*)

Finely chopped fresh chives or scallions (optional)

1. Scrub the beets thoroughly. Cook with bay leaves in water to cover for about 45 minutes, or until tender. Remove the bay leaves.

2. In a soup pot, melt the butter or heat the olive oil. Add the onions, carrot, cabbage, beet greens, caraway seeds, and dill and saute until all the vegetables are very tender.

3. If the beet skins are tough, slip them off. If not, leave them on. Blend the cooked beets, beet water, and vegetables, adding more water if necessary to reach a good consistency.

4. Add the lemon juice, salt, and pepper.

5. Chill thoroughly. Taste and reseason.

6. Serve garnished with finely chopped chives or scallions. Add a dollop of sour cream on top of each bowl if desired.

YIELD: SERVES 6

Cold Cucumber Walnut Soup

A customer left her copy of this recipe on a table in Cabbagetown. We tried it right away and liked it.

    2 cucumbers, peeled and diced

    1 cup chopped walnuts

    1 tablespoon good olive oil

    ½ cup finely chopped fresh dill (Do not make this with dried dill.)

    4 cups yoghurt

    1 cup sour cream

    2 cups half-and-half

1. Mix the cucumbers, walnuts, olive oil, and dill together. Cover and place in the refrigerator for 2 hours.

2. Add the yoghurt, sour cream, and half-and-half.

3. Chill thoroughly before serving.

YIELD: SERVES 6

Breads

When I ran Cabbagetown we were one of the only restaurants in Ithaca, New York, that made our own bread. Every day we served eager customers big warm slabs of a new variation on whole-grain bread. Bread was the "heart" of Cabbagetown. Many customers came just for the soup, salad, and bread. To this day, some former employees can still recite the corn bread recipe from memory.

Since those days I have moved into making my own sourdough breads and am still developing variations on natural sourdough starters.

Homemade bread is always the heart of my kitchen. In this bread sampler chapter, besides the recipes for Cabbagetown Corn Bread and Sourdough Starter & Sourdough Bread, there are recipes for foolproof Grainy (whole wheat) Bread, quick and yummy Cheese Herb Biscuits, and fried Indian Parathas.

27 *Grainy Bread*

Grainy bread is a wheaty, full-bodied bread with just a touch of honey. It's perfect for everything—for toast in the morning, for open-face sandwiches, for eating with soups and salads, and for serving with dinner. This recipe makes two big loaves or three little ones. This is the basic bread recipe with complete instructions. The secret to getting a good-textured bread is to work with a fairly wet dough and to give it plenty of time to rise.

> 3 cups hot water
>
> ⅓ cup honey OR maple syrup (*vegan option*)
>
> 2 tablespoons active dry yeast
>
> 4 cups whole wheat bread flour
>
> 3 tablespoons cooking oil
>
> 2 ½ teaspoons salt
>
> About 2 cups whole wheat bread flour
>
> Cornmeal

1. Measure the water into a bread bowl. In it dissolve the honey or maple syrup, stirring with a wooden spoon.

2. Drop the yeast into the water while it is still warm. (The ideal water temperature is 110°. You can drip it on the underside of your wrist and the water will feel the same as your body temperature.) Leave the water-yeast mixture for about 5 minutes, while the yeast dissolves and begins to foam.

3. Gradually add the 4 cups whole wheat bread flour, stirring until the mixture is smooth.

4. Leave this "sponge" to rise in a warm spot for 1–2 hours, stirring it down once or twice as it gets high.

5. Pour in the oil around the edges of the bowl. Stir it in, along with the salt.

6. Gradually add more whole wheat flour, stirring in 1 direction all the time to work up gluten most effectively. You can watch the gluten forming. Those tiny stretching fibers are strands of gluten. They're made up of the proteins in the flour, which are kept separate from each other when the flour is dry. When you mix the flour with water, the proteins are brought together and begin to form the elastic gluten network.

The gluten will hold your bread together and give it the springy texture you're beginning to feel as you stir. Most importantly, when the yeast in your dough starts giving off carbon dioxide gas later, the gas will be trapped in pockets of gluten; they'll blow up like tiny balloons, causing your bread to rise.

The gluten strands in whole wheat bread can never get as long as those in white bread because the little flakes of bran in whole wheat flour have sharp edges and cut some of the gluten. If you look closely, you might be able to see that happening. Because bran cuts gluten, whole wheat bread is never as light and airy as white bread.

The more you stir, the more gluten will form, so don't be hesitant.

7. Turn the dough onto a lightly floured counter and knead for 5 minutes. Kneading builds up still more gluten than you've worked up by stirring; and kneading lines up the gluten strands to form the strong framework of pockets which will hold in the gas given off by the yeast. You can feel your dough getting more elastic as you knead and more gluten develops.

   To knead, fold the dough in half towards you—your right hand folding, your left hand pushing the dough in the center to help. (Left-handed people reverse the hands.) With the heels of both your palms on the edge of the dough nearest you, push the dough down and away from you. If you get the motion right, the dough will spring as you roll it. Retrieve the dough, put a little more flour on the board if the dough sticks, then turn the dough 90 degrees (one-quarter turn) and fold again. This process gets smooth, rhythmic. Watch your friends knead. It's beautiful.

   Be light-handed. Resist the temptation to knead in too much flour. The dough should continue to be sticky and hard to work with, since a slightly wet dough is best for gluten formation. Dust the counter with flour only as needed. You've kneaded enough when you can poke the dough with your thumb and the dough springs back.

8. Lightly oil the bread bowl and return the dough to it.

9. Allow the dough to rise in a warm spot for 1–2 hours, or until it is more than double in bulk. Punch it down.

continues . . .

10. Divide the dough into 2 or 3 portions, depending on the number of loaves you want. Knead each portion of dough until it holds together in a smooth ball. Leave the balls on a lightly floured counter to rise for 1–2 hours or until they're more than double in bulk.

11. Punch down. Shape each ball into a free-form loaf-shaped or round and arrange on cookie sheets sprinkled with cornmeal or shape and place in buttered or oiled (vegan) bread pans.

12. Let the loaves rise in a warm spot for about 45 minutes, or until double in bulk.

13. Slash with a serrated knife in a decorative pattern (this will allow the steam to escape during baking).

14. Place the loaves in a preheated 350° oven. Bake until the loaves are firm and golden brown, and sound hollow when tapped on the bottom. Large loaves bake in about 60 minutes. Smaller loaves bake in 40–50 minutes.

15. Remove from the pans and allow to cool on cooling racks.

YIELD: 2 OR 3 LOAVES

Sourdough Starter & Sourdough Bread

Sourdough bread baking is currently my greatest interest in the kitchen.

Sourdough Starter

You're in your house. You've heard about sourdough bread. You want to make it. What do you do? First, have patience. It's a 5 day process from when you begin to make the starter to when the bread comes out of the oven. But you only need to make the starter once or occasionally. Once you have a starter, making the bread itself is still a 1–2 day process, and well worth it!

There are many ways of getting a sourdough starter. You can get a tried and true sourdough starter culture from a friend. You can start your culture going from dried starter (available in specialty and natural foods stores, and actually quite good). You can also make a culture from the air, as in this recipe. Or you can make a starter using the culture on ripe, unsprayed grapes. These cultures are exceptionally fine and are quite vigorous. My current starter comes from organic pinot noir grapes of my friend's vineyard on Seneca Lake. So I've named this beautiful fragrant culture Seneca Sourdough.

> **3 cups organic unbleached white flour**
> **Pinch (1/16 teaspoon) dried baker's yeast**
> **2¼ cups lukewarm water**

Day 1: Begin the starter

1. Get out your unbleached organic white flour. (*Organic* because some of the yeast that adheres to the outside of the wheat berry gets through to the culture. *White* because the culture is more adaptable if started in white flour, which has no problems with rancidity, no oil to spoil.) Mix 1 cup white flour with ¾ cup water and a pinch (1/16 teaspoon) of dried baker's yeast in a ceramic (non-metal) bowl.

continues . . .

—

2. Stir 100 strokes, to incorporate air. The baker's yeast you've used to start the culture isn't going to live long. It simply advertises that here's a great place for natural yeasts and other micro-organisms. The conditions of fermentation (in the starter culture) favor these new organisms. The more acidic your sourdough culture becomes, the less favorable to regular old baking yeast.

3. Cover the bowl with a plate—but not tightly. Air needs to be able to circulate in and out, but you don't want stuff to drop in. Leave the wooden stirring spoon in to guarantee air flow. Leave in a place that's 75° to 80°. (In summer this could be a dark cupboard, in winter near your stove or wood stove.) Your sourdough culture should begin bubbling a bit.

Day 2: Starter continued

4. To what you have, mix in another 1 cup white flour and ¾ cup water. Stir 100 strokes to incorporate air. Put the plate back on the bowl, with the spoon in. Put back in your 75° to 80° place for 24 more hours.

Day 3: Starter continued

5. By now your sourdough starter should have a distinctly sour smell and a large part of the surface should be covered with bubbles. Throw out half. Add another 1 cup flour and ¾ cup water. Again, stir 100 strokes to incorporate air, put the plate back on the bowl with the spoon in, and replace in your 75° to 80° place for 24 hours more. After this time you should have a fragrant bubbling sourdough starter, ready to use.

Maintaining your sourdough culture

Once you get the sourdough starter culture going, keep it at room temperature and "feed" it once every day to keep it good and active. Feeding the culture means build it up to double its volume by adding equal volumes of flour and water. Stir 100 strokes. Then pour off half of it and discard in your compost. If you aren't using your starter regularly, keep it in the refrigerator. Take it out and feed it once a week. *Warning*—this is often not good for the culture (some of the organisms may die in the refrigerator and you'll lose the rich flavors of the starter culture). If this happens start over again.

Sourdough Starter from Organic Grapes

Tie ½–1 pound grapes in a sheet of cheesecloth. Right at the beginning when you are mixing flour, water, and yeast, squeeze the juice out of the grapes into that mixture as per the recipe, and stir it in. When you leave your starter to rest, put the cheesecloth bag of grapes right in the bowl with the starter, and leave the bag of grapes in as the starter develops. Remove the bag after the starter gets going (about the third day).

Sourdough Bread

I recommend that you do try this sourdough bread-making schedule because the results are extraordinary and predictable. But if you're like me, you can make excellent sourdough bread with any timing on the two rises that suits your fancy. This recipe makes 1 nice big sourdough loaf or 2 smaller ones. Fresh-baked sourdough bread is delicious with everything!

    2 cups sourdough starter

    6 cups unbleached organic white flour

    2 cups whole wheat bread flour

    3 cups lukewarm water

    2 teaspoons salt

    Extra white flour for kneading

    Vegetable oil for oiling bread bowl

    Cornmeal for sprinkling on baking pan

Day 1: Mixing dough day

1. Enjoy your day at work. It's evening. You've had dinner. You're ready to go. Measure out 2 cups of your sourdough culture for use in making your bread dough. Feed the remaining culture and put it aside.

continues . . .

2. Mix together your flours in a big and shallow (so you can knead in it) ceramic bowl. You'll have better success with mostly white flour and a little whole wheat flour. The bran in whole wheat flour cuts gluten. This gets in the way of big bubbles and makes sourdough bread denser. Particularly in sourdough bread you want big bubbles and a light loaf. Make a well in the center of the flour mixture.

3. In a separate bowl mix the 2 cups starter with 3 cups water.

4. Pour liquid starter mix into the well of flour. Stir with wooden spoon. Beat 100 strokes to build serious gluten.

5. Either turn the bread dough onto a table or knead it in the bowl. Continue kneading in more flour. The dough should remain sticky. Have courage! The pain and suffering you're dealing with in working with a sticky dough will get you the big bubbles you're looking for. (The stickiness of the dough varies with exactly what flour you use. You'll learn from experience how much flour to use.) Knead for 10 minutes.

6. Sprinkle the 2 teaspoons salt over the dough and knead it in. The salt will firm up the gluten and instantly the bread dough will become less sticky. Knead 5 minutes more. Coat the bowl with oil and put dough in the oiled bowl.

7. Put a big plate or cookie tray over the bowl.

8. Leave overnight at 75° (ideal temperature). If the house is really cold, put the covered bowl with the dough near your stove or woodstove or in the oven with pilot light on. Leave overnight.

Day 2: Shaping and baking day

9. In the morning shape one or two round loaves. The dough should hold its shape. If it doesn't, knead in flour until it does. For classic loaves, put your shaped loaves in well-floured bowls or baskets. (Flour the bowl or basket *very well* so the dough won't stick.) Or put the shaped loaves directly on baking trays sprinkled with cornmeal.

10. Leave the loaves in a coolish place (60° is ideal, but 75° to 80° is okay) to rise all day, or at least 6 to 8 hours until late afternoon or early evening.

This long rise after the dough is shaped is called proofing. (If after 6 to 8 hours the dough has completely lost its shape, you probably didn't add enough flour in step 9. Knead in a little more—just enough to restore the loaf's integrity—reshape, and proof 2 more hours.)

11. After the proofing, preheat the oven to 425° and put a pan of water in the bottom for steam.

12. If you've proofed in bowls or baskets turn the loaves out onto baking trays sprinkled with cornmeal. Loaves proofed on baking trays are ready to go. Slash the loaves with a very sharp knife or a razor blade in a pattern you like. I like to slash mine 5 times in the pattern of outstretched fingers.

13. Put the loaves into the oven. Bake for 15 minutes at 425°. Then turn the oven down to 350° and bake the loaves 30–40 minutes more or until they're done. To give your sourdough a thicker crust you can spray water with a spray bottle into the oven once or twice as you bake. Loaves are done when they sound hollow when they're tapped on the bottom.

14. Remove from the baking trays and cool on racks.

Sourdough Bread with Currants or Raisins

1 cup dried currants or raisins

1 cup warm water

Use *2 cups* white flour plus *4 cups* whole wheat bread flour. Soak the dried currants or raisins in the warm water for 1 hour or more, then pour off soaking water. Knead in these plumped currants or raisins in step 6. The crazy good taste of whole wheat sourdough with raisins or currants makes up for the denser bread.

YIELD: ONE 4-5 POUND ROUND LOAF OR

TWO 2+ POUND ROUND LOAVES

Cabbagetown Corn Bread

This corn bread is famous throughout the greater Ithaca area, and anywhere Ithacans have traveled. For seven years I tried to scale down our restaurant recipe to a home-size version. This is very close. Use the freshest cornmeal you can get and be sure to use whole wheat *pastry* flour.

1 ¼ cups cornmeal

¾ cup whole wheat pastry flour

¼ cup dried milk powder

1 teaspoon salt

2 teaspoons baking powder

1 egg

¼ cup honey

1 cup milk

3 tablespoons light vegetable oil

1. In a medium-size bowl, mix together the cornmeal, flour, milk powder, and salt. Mix in the baking powder, rubbing it between your hands as you add it so there are no lumps.

2. Make a well in the center of the dry ingredients, and in it beat the egg lightly. Mix the honey, milk, and oil into the egg.

3. Mix the wet ingredients into the dry, and beat thoroughly so the batter is smooth and there are no lumps.

4. Pour the batter into a well-buttered 9-inch pie pan. Bake in a preheated 350° oven for 25–30 minutes, until the corn bread is firm and lightly browned. Serve warm from the oven with plenty of butter.

5. Often variations in the kinds of cornmeal and pastry flour you use will cause variation in the final texture of the corn bread. If you make this recipe once and the corn bread is dry, try adding more milk to the batter. If the corn bread is too wet and dense, add more cornmeal.

YIELD: ONE 9-INCH ROUND CORN BREAD

Vegan Corn Bread

Make the batter for the Classic Vegan Corn Muffins (page 118) or Vegan Corn Muffins with Fennel Seeds (page 120) and pour into an oiled 9-inch by 13-inch baking dish. Bake in a preheated 350° oven for 30–35 minutes until firm and lightly browned.

YIELD: ONE 9-INCH BY 13-INCH CORN BREAD

Cheese Herb Biscuits

These biscuits are quick and easy to make, and very flavorful.

2 cups whole wheat pastry flour

2 teaspoons baking powder

½ teaspoon salt

½ teaspoon dried basil or 1 teaspoon finely chopped fresh basil

½ teaspoon dried or finely chopped fresh thyme

¼ cup cold butter

½ pound cheddar or swiss cheese, grated (2 cups)

¾ cup milk or buttermilk

1. In a medium-size bowl, mix together the dry ingredients.

2. Grate in the butter. Toss it in with a fork. Then toss in the grated cheese. Mix in the milk or buttermilk.

3. Knead the dough in the bowl until it holds together. If it doesn't hold together, add a little more liquid. Form into 8–10 balls, flatten each ball a bit, and place on an ungreased cookie sheet.

4. Bake in a preheated 350° oven for about 25 minutes, or until lightly browned. Serve at once while still hot.

YIELD: 8-10 BISCUITS

arathas

These are rich Indian flat breads, made with oil in the dough. A friend says that in India when girls start learning to roll out parathas, they always try for a round shape. Since you can get them round only with years of practice, you can easily tell the inexperienced cooks—their parathas are shaped like India.

1 cup whole wheat bread flour

1 cup whole wheat pastry flour

1 teaspoon salt

About ¾ cup cold water

Whole wheat pastry flour for dusting the counter

½ cup finely chopped scallions

Light vegetable oil

1. Mix the flours with the salt in a medium-size mixing bowl. Add cold water until you get a kneadable dough. Knead the dough on a lightly floured counter until the dough sticks together. Divide it into lemon-size balls.

2. Roll out the balls 1 at a time as follows, dusting the counter with flour only as needed. First roll out the dough until it is the size of a small saucer. Put a teaspoon of oil on it, and smooth the oil over the surface. Sprinkle with 1 tablespoon chopped scallions. Fold the paratha in half and press the edges. Fold in half again. (Now it is wedge-shaped.) Roll out the wedge to 4 times its size, aiming for a final round shape.

3. Heat a cast iron frying pan. Put in 1 paratha and roast it for a couple of minutes on both sides. Add 1 teaspoon oil to the pan and roast each side again until brown spots appear. Taste your first paratha to make sure it's done. Sometimes the paratha puffs up. They may not puff up for novices— but as you gain experience, they will. Continue to roast all the parathas. Serve immediately.

YIELD: 6–8 PARATHAS.

SERVES 6

Salads & Dressings

Salads are the glory of life. In the
summer I always recommend a mixed green salad with all the
wonderful new lettuces that are available, as well as arugula,
mitzuna, radicchio, or mesclun salad mix.

The salad dressings I have chosen for this chapter are
legendary. People have come up to me across the country
to rave about the Rugged Garlic, Yoghurt Tahini, and
Lemon Sesame dressings. Any of these dressings can be
used on a tossed mixed green salad, on cooked vegetables,
or on the Wings of Life Salad. Some people have even
been known to eat them with a spoon.

Since leaving Cabbagetown, I've run a vegetarian deli for two
years and have come to enjoy the enormous variety of
vegetarian "deli" salads—composed salads made from pasta or
potatoes, different vegetables, grains, beans, and dressings.
Several deli salads—such as the Vietnamese Pasta Salad,
Mexican Potato Salad, or the One World Salad—with a good
loaf of bread and some herb butter or olive oil, make a great
picnic meal indoors or indoors. I eat this way often.

At home if I don't have a green salad with a meal, I make the
quick and simple Quick Blanched Vegetables with my
Fresh Lemon & Garlic Dressing. Since cooked vegetables can
be incorporated into many salads, and blanching vegetables is
an art, I'm including it. Herbed Baked Tofu is another
great salad addition.

Lemon Sesame Dressing

Lemon Sesame Dressing is light and fresh, and I can't resist the sesame flavor.

¼ cup sesame seeds

1 cup light vegetable oil

Juice of 2 lemons

2 tablespoons red wine vinegar

1 tablespoon tamari or soy sauce

1 cup lightly packed fresh green herbs (chives, scallions, parsley, basil, dill)

½ teaspoon salt

½ teaspoon mustard powder

1 teaspoon dried thyme or finely chopped fresh thyme

¼ teaspoon dried or fresh whole rosemary

1. Toast the sesame seeds over low heat in a frying pan until they're lightly browned. Be careful not to burn them.

2. Measure all the ingredients including the toasted sesame seeds into the blender and blend until smooth.

3. Taste on a vegetable stick and adjust the seasonings if needed.

YIELD: 2 CUPS

Yoghurt Tahini Dressing

Yoghurt Tahini was the faithful salad dressing at Cabbagetown. Use it as a dip for raw and steamed vegetables, and as a dressing for sandwiches in pita bread. Try crumbled feta cheese in any tossed salad with this dressing.

1 cup plain yoghurt

½ cup tahini

Juice of 1 lemon

1 clove of garlic, finely chopped

¼ teaspoon salt

2 tablespoons finely chopped fresh parsley

1 tablespoon finely chopped fresh chives or scallions (optional)

1. With a whisk, mix together all the ingredients until smooth.

2. Taste on a vegetable stick. You might want to add more lemon juice.

YIELD: 1 ½ CUPS

Rugged Garlic Dressing

This is the dressing some Cabbagetown customers made jokes about.
"Oh dear," a young Cornell student once said glancing at her boyfriend,
"I'll have the garlic dressing if you do." This dressing tastes especially good
on salads with croutons and big leaves of fresh spinach.

> 4–6 cloves garlic
>
> ½ cup lightly packed fresh green herbs (chives, scallions, parsley, basil, dill)
>
> 1 egg
>
> ½ teaspoon salt
>
> 1 tablespoon red wine vinegar
>
> 1 cup light vegetable oil
>
> ¼ cup red wine vinegar
>
> ½ teaspoon black pepper

1. If you're using a whisk, finely chop the garlic and fresh green herbs. If you're using a blender, you can add them whole and the blender will chop them.

2. Whisk or blend the egg with the salt, 1 tablespoon vinegar, and the garlic until creamy.

3. Whisking or blending constantly, add about ½–⅔ cup of the oil in a slow trickle. At some point the dressing will take and become much thicker.

4. After it thickens, continue beating in the remaining oil alternately with the ¼ cup vinegar.

5. Whisk or blend in the herbs and pepper.

6. Taste on a vegetable stick and adjust the seasonings if needed.

7. If the dressing doesn't take—if it breaks into separate oil and vinegar layers —whisk or blend another egg and add the dressing to the egg, whisking or blending constantly as you did with the oil. If this still doesn't work, just use the dressing as it is. It will have the consistency of a vinaigrette.

Tofu Rugged Garlic

Use ½ pound tofu instead of egg. The dressing won't "take" as an egg mayonnaise does but it will be thick and delicious.

YIELD: 1 ½ CUPS

35 Steve's Tofu Dressing

This creamy dressing is subtly flavored with dark sesame oil, tahini, and dill. It's a good way to introduce people to tofu.

½ cup crumbled tofu

¼ cup water

2 tablespoons tahini

2 tablespoons light vegetable oil

2 tablespoons red wine vinegar

1 tablespoon tamari or soy sauce

1 teaspoon dried dill weed or 1 tablespoon finely chopped fresh dill

1 teaspoon dark sesame oil

1 clove of garlic, finely chopped

1. Measure all the ingredients into the blender and blend until smooth.

2. Taste on a vegetable stick and adjust the seasonings if needed.

YIELD: I CUP

36 Tarragon Vinaigrette Dressing

This is a very simple dressing. Because it is so simple, the quality of the ingredients you use makes a big difference. Get the best olive oil and the best french mustard you can. If you can find it, fresh tarragon is better than dried. This dressing tastes especially good on salads with one or more of the following ingredients: avocados, cooked lentils, tender lettuces, crumbled blue cheese, croutons, or cooked pasta.

¾ cup olive oil

Juice of 1 lemon

1 tablespoon red wine vinegar

1 tablespoon prepared french mustard

2 cloves of garlic, finely chopped

1 teaspoon dried tarragon or ½ teaspoon finely chopped fresh tarragon

½ teaspoon salt

½ teaspoon freshly ground black pepper

1. Mix together all the ingredients.

2. Taste on a vegetable stick and adjust the seasonings if needed.

Fresh Herb Vinaigrette

Add 1 teaspoon of any chopped fresh herbs in addition to the tarragon. Good herbs to use are parsley, dill, chives, basil. Use a comparatively lesser amount of stronger herbs such as thyme, oregano, rosemary.

YIELD: I CUP

Julie's Fresh Lemon & Garlic Dressing

I put this dressing on everything I eat. I use it on green salads, grains, pastas, cooked greens—everything!

6 cloves garlic

Juice of 2 lemons

½ teaspoon sea salt

½ cup olive oil

1 teaspoon good prepared french mustard (optional)

Freshly ground black pepper (optional)

1. Chop the garlic finely. Getting the exact right-sized pieces is an art.

2. Marinate the garlic in lemon juice for 10–15 minutes to soften the acidity of the garlic.

3. Using a whisk or fork, mix the salt and olive oil into the garlic-lemon mixture.

4. Whisk in the mustard if you choose.

5. Toss this dressing with a large green salad. If desired, top off the dressed salad or other food with a bit of freshly ground black pepper from your pepper mill.

YIELD: ¾–I CUP

Creamy Lemon Mayonnaise

Occasionally I make salads with 2 dressings. I spread Creamy Lemon Mayonnaise on the salad plate, then top it with a green salad tossed with a light dressing like Tarragon Vinaigrette or Julie's Fresh Lemon & Garlic dressing. Such a combination is extravagant and delicious. Add this mayonnaise to potato salads, or pasta salads. Serve it as a dip for boiled new potatoes, blanched green beans, broccoli, and cauliflower.

> 2 cloves of garlic
>
> 1 tablespoon dried green herbs or ½–1 cup lightly packed fresh green herbs (Chives, basil, dill, parsley, and scallions are all good choices.)
>
> 1 egg
>
> ½ teaspoon salt
>
> 1 tablespoon red wine vinegar
>
> 1 cup light vegetable oil
>
> Juice of 1 lemon
>
> 1 tablespoon prepared french mustard
>
> ½ teaspoon black pepper

1. If you're using a whisk, finely chop the garlic and the fresh green herbs. If you're using a blender, you can add them whole and the blender will chop them.

2. Whisk or blend the egg with the salt, vinegar, and garlic until creamy.

3. Whisking or blending constantly, add about ½–⅔ cup of oil in a slow trickle. At some point the mayonnaise will "take" and become much thicker.

4. After it thickens, continue beating or blending in the remaining oil alternately with the lemon juice.

5. Whisk or blend in the mustard, pepper, and herbs.

6. Taste on a vegetable stick and adjust the seasonings if needed.

YIELD: 2 CUPS

Wings of Life Salad

One day a staff member of Cabbagetown Café asked, "Why don't we serve the customers what the staff eats?" Thus was born the Wings of Life Salad, named after my first cookbook, *Wings of Life*. This salad is a whole meal. You might want to serve bread and butter or small cups of soup with it, but it can stand on its own.

2 cups Herbed Baked Tofu (page 51)

6 cups blanched broccoli (See Blanched Vegetables steps 1–5 on page 50.)

1 cup cashews or Tamari-Roasted Almonds (page 3)

½ pound swiss or feta or cottage cheese

   OR 1 cup cooked brown rice (*vegan option*)

Salad greens and vegetables

Alfalfa sprouts, finely grated carrots, or finely grated beets

Your favorite salad dressing (pages 44–48)

1. Prepare the tofu. Allow to cool.

2. Prepare broccoli. Allow to cool.

3. Toast the cashews in a 350° oven or toaster oven for about 15–20 minutes, or until lightly browned. Be careful not to burn them.

4. Grate the swiss cheese, or crumble the feta (if you are using them).

5. Prepare a base of fresh salad greens, including any chopped or grated fresh vegetables you like.

6. Toss the tofu cubes, the steamed broccoli, the nuts, and the grated or crumbled cheeses (or the brown rice) into the salad greens. If you're using cottage cheese, put it on top of the salad greens around the edges. Top with alfalfa sprouts, grated carrots, or grated beets (or all 3).

7. At the last minute toss the salad with your choice of a salad dressing and serve. Or serve the salad undressed and let each person put on his or her own dressing.

YIELD: SERVES 4

Quick Blanched Vegetables with Fresh Lemon & Garlic Dressing

At every meal I have either a green salad or hot blanched vegetables with a dressing. Long ago, before I understood blanching, I steamed vegetables. Now there's no comparison. Blanching gives cooked vegetables the best flavors, colors, and textures. My Fresh Lemon & Garlic Dressing is the perfect light and zingy accompaniment.

> **Some Favorite Vegetables to Blanch (Choose 1 or more.)**
>> 1 head broccoli or cauliflower
>>
>> Big bunch kale
>>
>> Big bunch mustard greens
>>
>> Bowlful (1 pound) green beans
>>
>> Big bunch asparagus
>>
>> Bowlful (1 pound) brussels sprouts
>>
>> Bowlful (1 pound) sugar snap peas or snow peas
>
> Water
>
> Julie's Fresh Lemon & Garlic Dressing (page 47)

1. Prepare the vegetable. Wash. Cut in bite-sized pieces. With broccoli I always use the stem, but peel it because it's woody.

2. Fill a medium-large pot with water. Bring to a boil.

3. Drop vegetables into the boiling water. If you're cooking a lot of vegetables, do them in batches. Add only enough vegetables so the water becomes quiet for an instant when you add the vegetables then quickly comes back to a boil. The energy of blanching is very active and quick.

4. The vegetable is just-cooked when some of the starches in the vegetable are broken down to sugars by the heat. Green vegetables such as broccoli or kale will turn bright green. Non-green vegetables will suddenly become brighter, more shiny. The best test is to pull out 1 piece of a vegetable and bite it. It will taste sweet, delicious, and be crisp but not crunchy.

5. As soon as the vegetables are just cooked, lift them immediately out of the water with a wire-mesh wok spoon or a slotted spoon. Put batches in a beautiful serving bowl.

6. Drizzle with Julie's Fresh Lemon & Garlic Dressing.

YIELD: SERVES 1–4

Herbed Baked Tofu

This is the way I prepare tofu for use in salads and stir-fries. There's lots of flavor in the tofu cubes.

2 tablespoons olive oil

1 pound tofu, cut in bite-size cubes (2 cups)

2–4 cloves of garlic, finely chopped

½ teaspoon freshly ground black pepper

1 teaspoon dried dill weed or 2 tablespoons freshly chopped fresh dill

Pinch cayenne

1 teaspoon dark sesame oil

2 teaspoons tamari or soy sauce

1. Oil a baking pan with the olive oil. Cover with tofu cubes.

2. Sprinkle with the garlic, black pepper, dill, cayenne, sesame oil, and tamari or soy sauce.

3. Bake in a 350° oven for about 30 minutes, lifting and stirring with a spatula once or twice so the tofu cubes are evenly browned and crisped.

4. Remove from the oven and adjust the seasonings.

YIELD: 2 CUPS.

SERVES 4 IN SALADS OR STIR-FRIES

Vietnamese Pasta Salad

The traditional Vietnamese Pasta Salad was brought to us at Cabbagetown by Loan, our loving and talented Vietnamese cook. I adapted it for the very popular deli version when I ran the Whole Earth Deli in Princeton, New Jersey. The traditional salad is made with Asian rice noodles, while the deli-style version includes cooked spiral pasta.

Vietnamese Dressing (step 1)
½ cup lime juice
⅓ cup tamari or soy sauce
2 tablespoons sesame oil
½ cup light vegetable oil
½ tablespoon honey OR rice syrup (*vegan option*)
½ teaspoon fresh grated ginger
⅛ teaspoon ground szechuan pepper (optional)

Sweet & Sour Carrots (step 2)
3 cups packed, grated carrots
¼ cup lemon juice
1 teaspoon honey OR rice syrup (*vegan option*)
1 ½ teaspoons salt

Tofu (step 3)
3 pounds (3 blocks) tofu, each sliced into 3 rectangular slabs
1 cup light vegetable oil (if deep frying) or
   2 tablespoons of sesame oil (if baking)
5 cloves garlic, finely chopped
1 ½ cups onions, finely chopped
1 heaping teaspoon fresh grated ginger
1 teaspoon dried chiles or chopped hot pepper
5 tablespoons tamari

Pasta: Choose *one* of the following pastas. (step 4)

> 1 pound Asian rice noodles (Soak the rice noodles in a bowl of warm water until they are soft, at least 20–30 minutes before they are needed. Drain before using.)
>
> 1 pound whole grain spiral pasta (Sesame rice spirals are great.) Cook according to How to Cook Pasta on page 89.

Garnishes (step 5)

> ½ cup scallions, chopped
>
> ½ cup roasted peanuts, chopped
>
> Salad greens (for traditional Vietnamese Pasta Salad)

1. **Vietnamese Dressing.** Whisk all ingredients for the Vietnamese dressing together in a medium size mixing bowl. Store in a quart container. This dressing can be made well ahead of time and stored in the refrigerator.

2. **Sweet & Sour Carrots.** Mix all the sweet & sour carrots ingredients together. Marinate 1 hour. Squeeze out the liquid and discard it.

3. **Tofu.** Deep fry tofu slices in very hot oil until golden brown, or bake in a 375° oven on sheet trays coated with sesame oil until they start to crisp, about 20–30 minutes. Drain and cool. Then slice into thin strips. Saute with remaining ingredients in a wok or frying pan.

4. **Pasta.** If using rice noodles, drain at this time. If using spiral pasta, cook according to How to Cook Pasta, but instead of olive oil, toss the pasta with a little dressing or with toasted sesame oil after cooking.

5. **Assembly.** For traditional Vietnamese Pasta Salad, put piles of rice noodles, carrots, and tofu on top of salad greens. Sprinkle with chopped scallions and roasted peanuts. Serve with dressing on the side. For deli Vietnamese Pasta Salad, mix cooked spiral pasta with dressing, carrots, tofu, and scallions. Sprinkle with chopped roasted peanuts.

YIELD: SERVES 4–6

Szechuan Noodles

This classic, spicy Chinese noodle salad is very quick and easy to make, and pleases everyone.

Szechuan Dressing (step 1)
½ cup tahini
½ cup water
½ cup tamari
½ cup lemon juice
4 cloves garlic, finely chopped
¼ cup dark sesame oil
¼ teaspoon cayenne pepper

Pasta & Vegetables (steps 2, 3)
1 pound udon or linguine noodles
1 tablespoon toasted sesame oil (*vegan option*)
2 medium cucumbers, peeled
8 scallions

1. Mix the dressing ingredients together in a bowl with a wooden spoon.

2. Cook the noodles according to the directions in How to Cook Pasta (page 89). Toss the cooked pasta with toasted sesame oil instead of olive oil.

3. To chop the vegetables: Remove the inner seedy section of the cucumbers, especially if the seeds are large or the cucumbers old or oversized. Cut the cucumbers into half-moon slices. Cut the scallions diagonally.

4. Gently mix all the ingredients together.

5. Serve immediately or store in the refrigerator until serving.

YIELD: SERVES 4–6

Mexican Potato Salad

This salad is very good plain, as a dip for tortilla chips, or as a filling
for tostadas and tacos.

3 potatoes

¼ cup butter OR olive oil (*vegan option*)

2 cups fresh or frozen corn

½ cup cashews

½ cup sunflower seeds

1 tablespoon ground cumin

2 teaspoons ground coriander

1 onion, chopped

1 cup chopped black olives

¼ cup finely chopped fresh chives or scallions

1 cup sour cream (*optional, non-vegan*)

1 teaspoon salt

1. Scrub the potatoes well, but do not peel. Cook in water to cover until just
   tender, about 30 minutes after the water boils. Do not overcook. The
   easiest way to tell if a potato is done is to spear it with a knife. Dice into
   bite-size cubes.

2. Cook the vegetables in 2 steps to avoid overcooking anything, and to ensure
   the separate, crisp texture of each salad ingredient. Heat half (2 tablespoons)
   of the butter or olive oil in a medium-size frying pan. Add the corn, cashews,
   sunflower seeds, and half the spices. Saute for 4–5 minutes, until the corn is
   lightly cooked. Remove to a large bowl.

3. Heat the remaining (2 tablespoons) butter or olive oil in the frying pan.
   Add the onion, the cooked potato cubes, and the remaining spices. Saute
   until the onions are tender. Add to the other vegetables in the bowl.

4. While the vegetables are still hot, mix in the olives, chives or scallions, sour
   cream (if using) and salt. Taste and reseason if necessary.

5. Serve immediately or store in the refrigerator until serving.

YIELD: SERVES 4

Darryl's Pasta Salad

Darryl was the name of our salad refrigerator at Cabbagetown Café. A friend named Darryl had been to a conference and pasted his name tag to the refrigerator. The tag stuck. This dish is a great centerpiece for a picnic, good with crusty sourdough bread and a dry white wine or Zinfandel. Be sure to have a pepper grinder in the picnic basket.

1 pound pasta (Shells are good because they catch the dressing.)

1 cup Tarragon Vinaigrette Dressing (page 89)

½ teaspoon dried or finely chopped fresh tarragon

¼ teaspoon salt

1½ cups Tamari-Roasted Almonds (page 3)

1–2 cups freshly grated parmesan cheese (*optional, non-vegan*)

Salad greens and vegetables

½ cup alfalfa sprouts, sunflower sprouts, or nasturtium flowers

½ cup black olives

Your favorite salad dressing (pages 44–48)

1. Cook the pasta according to the instructions on How to Cook Pasta on page 89. After you've returned the pasta to the cooking pot, toss in the 1 cup of Tarragon-Vinaigrette dressing, the tarragon, and the salt. Allow to cool, tossing occasionally to blend the flavors.

2. Prepare the almonds and grate the cheese if you are using it.

3. Make a nest of your favorite salad greens and vegetables in a big salad bowl. If you want to go all out, add sliced raw mushrooms, sliced red onions, and sliced avocados.

4. Put the pasta in the center of the greens. Cover with a thick layer of parmesan cheese if you are using it, then sprinkle with the almonds, sprouts, or nasturtiums, and black olives.

5. Leave the salad this way for maximum scenic effect until you're ready to eat it. Then toss with your favorite salad dressing and serve. Or leave the salad undressed and let each person put on his or her own dressing.

YIELD: SERVES 4–6

German Cucumber Salad

The trick to making this German salad is to slice cucumbers and tomatoes so thin your grandmother would be proud of you. The German grandmother who taught me to make it was a tyrant. "It is impossible for Americans to make German salad," she told me when I tried. Eat this salad with a crusty bread which can be dunked in the salad juice.

> 3 cucumbers (If using store bought cucumbers peel them first.)
>
> 2 firm ripe tomatoes
>
> ½ cup Creamy Lemon Mayonnaise (page 48)
>
> 1–2 tablespoons lemon juice, to taste
>
> Salt to taste
>
> Freshly ground black pepper to taste
>
> 1–2 scallions, chopped

1. Cut the cucumbers and tomatoes into thin slices.

2. Add the mayonnaise to the vegetables and mix until coated.

3. Add lemon juice, salt, and pepper to taste.

4. Garnish salad with scallions and chill until serving.

YIELD: SERVES 4

One World Salad

This salad is good by itself or in pita bread with sprouts. It's called "one world" because it is universal in its appeal and ingredients—lentils, grains, tofu, veggies, and a wonderful dressing all in one salad.

Lentils (step 1)

    1 cup uncooked brown lentils

    ½ teaspoon thyme, dried or fresh

    1 bay leaf

    1 teaspoon olive oil

    3 cups water

Grains (step 2)

    ⅓ cup uncooked wild rice

    ¾ cup uncooked brown rice

    2 ¼ cups water

    Pinch sea salt

Dressing (step 3)

    3 medium-size cloves garlic, minced

    1 small or ½ large bell pepper, red or green, finely diced

    2 teaspoons thyme

    1 tablespoon salt

    ½ teaspoon pepper

    ½ cup olive oil

    2 tablespoons plus 1 teaspoon red wine vinegar

    ¼ cup lemon juice

    ½ pound tofu, finely diced

Vegetables (step 4)

    1 cup carrots

    1 cup celery

1 cup sunflower seeds, toasted (step 6)

1. Sort the lentils carefully for stones and rinse them. Combine the lentils in a medium-sized pot with the thyme, bay leaf, olive oil, and water. Bring to a boil. Then turn down to a simmer. Cook for about 45 minutes or until soft. Remove the bay leaf.

2. Cook the grains together according to instructions in How to Cook Grains on page 65.

3. While the lentils and grains are cooking, make the dressing. Mix all ingredients together in a bowl.

4. Finely dice the carrots and celery.

5. After they are cooked combine rice and lentils in a large bowl and cool completely to room temperature.

6. Toss the rice and lentils with the dressing, diced vegetables, and sunflower seeds. Taste and reseason.

7. Serve at room temperature or chilled.

YIELD: SERVES 6–8

Cucumber Raita

This is a cooling yoghurt salad to serve with an Indian meal.

1 teaspoon cumin seeds
2 cucumbers or tomatoes, chopped
    (Peel the cucumbers if they are store bought.)
1 red or white onion, cut in crescents
2 cups plain yoghurt
2 teaspoons finely chopped fresh mint
¼ teaspoon salt
¼ teaspoon paprika

1. Toast the cumin seeds lightly in a dry frying pan and mash them slightly with the back of a wooden spoon.

2. Mix together all the ingredients.

3. Taste and adjust the seasonings.

4. Refrigerate for 1–2 hours before serving. This raita does not keep well, so plan to eat it fresh.

YIELD: SERVES 6

Tabbouleh

The secret to this salad is the small amount of liquid, which leaves the bulghur flaky, not mushy. If you want the salad to be a whole meal, serve it with pita bread, black olives, and hummus.

2 cups uncooked bulghur

2 teaspoons salt

1 ½ cups boiling water

½ cup olive oil

Juice of 2 lemons

2 cloves of garlic, finely chopped

1 onion, diced

1 cucumber, diced (Peel if store bought.)

1 tomato, diced

1 tablespoon finely chopped fresh peppermint or spearmint

½ cup finely chopped fresh parsley

½ teaspoon black pepper

1. In a large bowl, mix the bulghur with the salt, then add the boiling water. Cover for 20 minutes, stirring occasionally.

2. Add the oil and lemon juice and let sit another 10 minutes.

3. Toss in the chopped vegetables, mint, parsley, and pepper. Marinate the salad in the refrigerator for several hours before serving, tossing it occasionally so the whole salad is covered with dressing.

YIELD: SERVES 4

50 Arame Green Bean Salad

This classic macrobiotic dish is strikingly beautiful, and really, really delicious. Green beans, snow peas, or sugar snap peas can be used. It can be served as a cold salad or as a hot vegetable dish.

1 ½ cup (dry measure) arame seaweed

Water to cover arame

1 medium onion, sliced

2–3 tablespoons toasted sesame oil, as needed for cooking the vegetables

2 cups carrots, sliced diagonally

2 cups fresh snow peas, green beans, or sugar snap peas, washed and
    stemmed

1 cup corn kernels, fresh or frozen (optional)

1–2 tablespoons tamari, as needed for seasoning

1. Soak the arame in water for at least half an hour.

2. Cook onion in sesame oil over low heat in a wok or frying pan until well wilted and golden brown. Pour into a large bowl.

3. Cook carrots in the same wok until soft and sweet. Add to the onions in the bowl.

4. Cook the snow peas, green beans, or sugar snap peas until they are tender-crisp. Add the corn (if using) and cook 1 minute. Transfer to bowl.

5. Pour off most of the arame soaking water (it is great for watering plants). Cook the arame seaweed with a little of the soaking water in the hot wok or frying pan. This will develop its deep flavor while "taking the edge off." Transfer the arame to the bowl.

6. Mix everything together. Season well with tamari.

YIELD: 6–8 SERVINGS

Koshimbir
Fresh Coconut Salad

This distinctive salad, with fresh coconut and peanut meal, is served in small bowls along with an Indian meal. Make it right before serving. You can chop the vegetables and prepare the coconut and peanut meal in advance, but don't toss the salad until the last instant. Also eat it all up at one sitting. The freshness and fun of it is totally lost on the second day.

> 1 cup grated fresh coconut
>
> 1 cup peanuts, raw or roasted
>
> 2 cucumbers, peeled and finely chopped
>
> 2 tomatoes, finely chopped
>
> Juice of 1 lemon
>
> 2 tablespoons light vegetable oil
>
> 1 teaspoon black mustard seeds
>
> Pinch asafetida
>
> Pinch turmeric
>
> 1 fresh hot pepper, finely chopped
>
> 1 teaspoon salt

1. Prepare the grated fresh coconut. Don't substitute dried coconut flakes. Be careful to choose coconuts without cracks and store them in the refrigerator. To crack them open, hit them on any hard surface like the front steps or the sidewalk (or use a hammer). Carefully use a knife to separate the coconut meat from the hard shell (this may require a little force). Grate the meat. Store any grated coconut you don't use immediately in the freezer in sealed plastic bags.

2. Make the peanuts into roasted peanut meal. If you're starting with raw peanuts, roast them in a dry frying pan for about 10 minutes, or until dark spots appear. Stir frequently so the peanuts don't burn. Allow to cool. Grind them in a grain mill, or at low speed in a blender or food processor. Don't grind too fast or you will make peanut butter. If you're starting with roasted peanuts, grind them as above.

3. With your hands, squeeze all the juice you can get out of the chopped cucumbers.

4. Mix together the coconut, peanut meal, cucumbers, tomatoes, and lemon juice.

5. In a small pot, heat the oil until a mustard seed dropped in it pops. Add the mustard seeds, asafetida, turmeric, and chopped hot pepper, and fry for about 30 seconds. Pour over the vegetable mixture. Mix in the salt.

6. Taste and adjust the seasonings. Chill in the refrigerator until serving.

Cabbage Koshimbir

Substitute a medium-size wedge of cabbage, very finely chopped, for 1 cucumber and 1 tomato.

YIELD: SERVES 6

Grains & Beans

The big change in my consciousness came the day I realized that for me the grain was the meal. If I didn't have a cooked grain, then I wasn't eating. I had gradually, without knowing it, switched from my early vegetarian bread and cheese and tomato based diet to a grain based diet. This is the traditional diet of the human, a central grain supplemented by vegetables, bits of rich food like cheese or meat, beans, condiments. No suffering, no pain. Just the excitement of the wide world of grains.

It is really glorious to be alive right now. Heirloom grains from all over the world are being rediscovered and grown again. The most obvious example is quinoa (pronounced "keenwa"), the staple grain of the Inca civilization. Now you can buy this smallish nutty and delightfully bitter grain, which cooks up to have a moon inside it, almost anywhere. There are also teff from Africa, amaranth the sacred grain of the Aztecs of Mexico, many varieties of corn and traditional ways of preparing it, wheat, which has been called the queen of grains in Europe, and countless varieties of rice grown all over the world. This is just the beginning.

The heirloom beans are spectacularly beautiful and delicious—Anasazi beans, chestnut lima beans, small black mitlas. Take a stroll down the beans aisle of the grocery store. You'll be amazed at all the beans—white, brown, red, black, speckled, spotted, in many shapes and sizes. Don't forget about lentils and split peas, too.

This chapter is just a tiny sampler of the wonderful world of grain and bean cooking. As I travel and try new grains and beans in their rediscovered settings I'm learning enough to write a whole travel and adventure cookbook. In this chapter I've included detailed instructions for cooking both grains and beans, the staples of life.

How to Cook Grains

Each grain is an energy and a culture. Each grain is a gift to our bodies, which become toned and healthier for eating grains.

In the winter I pressure-cook grains; in the summer I boil them. Occasionally I bake grains when the oven is going for something else. Baking is a great grain-cooking method in commercial settings because the ovens usually are on and because the timing is slower and not quite as crucial as cooking grains on top of the stove. You don't burn them.

General Instructions for Cooking Grains on the Stove

1. As a general rule wash all grains very thoroughly. Grains are usually dirty and need to be rinsed at least three times. To rinse, measure the grain into the cooking pot, cover with water, and swirl it around with your hand. Strain off the dirty water catching straying grains in a strainer. Do this 3 times.

2. In the pot, add water to your grain. With most rices and quinoa, the ratio of water to grain is between 1 ½–2 cups water to 1 cup grains. This often depends on how dry you like the grain. The ratio differs with millet where the ratio is 3 cups water to 1 cup millet and barley where it is anywhere from 3–5 cups water to 1 cup barley.

3. Always cook grains with a pinch of salt per cup of grain. Bring to boil over a medium to medium-high flame, add a pinch of sea salt per cup of grain, put on the lid, lower the heat, put the pot on a flame-tamer (or low simmer) and cook for 50 minutes or until water is absorbed.

4. At the end of 50 minutes, I stand in front of the grain, turn the flame up to full, take three deep breaths, then turn the heat off. This ritual actually gives the cooked grains a lovely texture. I let the grain sit covered for 15–20 minutes before serving. This gives the grains an extra fluffiness.

5. Scoop out of pot into wooden bowl, being sure to reach down to bottom of pot with each scoop to get the denser bottom grains and the lighter top grains together.

6. A good way to keep grains warmed and moist until serving is to cover them with a sushi mat.

continues . . .

Pressure-Cooked Grains

Use exactly the same method as boiled grains, but put on pressure-cooking lid instead of regular lid. Cook same amount of time.

Baking Grains in the Oven

Use the same ratio of water and grain and salt. Bake in a *covered* baking or casserole dish in a preheated 350° oven for the same amount of time as or up to 15–30 minutes longer than in the stove-top cooking instructions. The grains are done when all the water is absorbed.

Toasting Grains

I always toast buckwheat and sometimes toast millet, and rarely toast anything else although it is certainly possible. You toast a grain after you wash it. Put the pot with the washed grain over a medium flame, and stir the grain pretty constantly first while it dries and later as it begins to toast. If anything seems to be happening fast or is alarming, turn down the heat. As the grain toasts it will begin to brown very lightly and smell fragrant. It's done when it's mostly lightly browned. Toasting adds a nutty and deeper quality to the flavor of the cooked grain.

How Much Water to Cook a Grain

There is a whole range of textures available to you from the same grain depending on how much water you decide to cook it in. The usual way of discussing this is to talk about how many cups of water to 1 cup of grain. For instance if you add 2 cups of water to 1 cup of rice, you'd be cooking what we all grew up with as normal rice. If you cooked rice 1½ cup of water to 1 cup of rice you'd get chewy rice. You could cook rice 5 to 1, to get very soft rice gruel, which you could put through a Foley food mill to make rice cream.

The best way to learn this is to experiment. But as a general rule somewhere between 1 ½ cups water to 1 cup grain and 2 cups water to 1 cup grain will give you what you're used to for most grains.

Mixing grains

(Sample blended basmati rice recipes are on page 73.)

I usually cook one grain by itself, but I often enjoy a mixture of two grains. Mixing grains is a big part of my art. Perhaps it's because of my early training as an ice cream taster for my father, but I have an unusually finely honed appreciation for "mouth feel"—how grains mixed give some spectacular mouth feels (and tastes). I particularly like brown rice and millet, and white rice blended with other grains.

Goma Shio
Sesame Salt Condiment for Grains

If you haven't heard about the condiment goma shio for grains, let me clue you in. It's spectacular. It's lightly roasted sesame seeds ground together with salt to make a nutty, fragrant, salty condiment which magically enhances the natural flavors of the grains.

1 tablespoon sea salt

18 tablespoons (1 cup plus 2 tablespoons) unhulled sesame seeds

1. Roast the salt lightly in a large frying pan, stirring so it doesn't burn. Remove. Add the sesame seeds and roast over medium heat, stirring so they don't burn. They're done when they're fragrant, and when if you pick up a few and rub them between your thumb and forefinger they rub apart rather than staying intact.

2. Put the salt and sesame seeds in a mortar and pestle if you have one. If not use a blender or food processor. Grind or pulse them until the sesame seeds are about half pulverized. You still want some texture left.

3. Store in a glass jar with a tight fitting lid.

YIELD: 1 ¼–1 ½ CUPS

Millet with Vegetables

Millet cooks up very well with vegetables. Here are some special dishes I cook over and over again.

Millet with Squash

Sweet and creamy.

> 2 cups uncooked millet
> 2 cups kabocha, butternut, or other winter squash
> 6 cups water
> 1 teaspoon salt
> Chopped parsley

1 Cut the squash into 1-inch cubes. All commercial squash needs to be peeled because the skins are waxed. Homegrown or organic squash such as butternut or kabocha with soft skins don't need to be peeled and their skins soften entirely during cooking.

2. Wash the millet in a large pot. Add diced squash, water, and salt.

3. Bring to a boil. Turn heat down to low and let simmer, covered, until well cooked, about 20–30 minutes.

4. Let stand for 10 minutes before serving. You can serve this as is, or mash it with a potato masher or in a food processor.

5. Sprinkle with chopped fresh parsley.

Millet with Cauliflower

This classic grain dish is great!

> 1 head cauliflower, cut into small pieces
> 2 small onions or 1 large onion, diced
> 2 tablespoons olive oil
> 2 cups uncooked millet
> 6 cups water
> 1 teaspoon salt

1. Saute the cauliflower and onions in olive oil in a medium-size frying pan until they just start to get soft.

2. Wash the millet in a large pot. Add cooked cauliflower and onions, water, and salt.

3. Bring to boil. Turn heat down to low and let simmer, covered, until well cooked, about 20–30 minutes.

4. Let stand 10 minutes before serving. You can serve this as is, or mash it with a potato masher or in a food processor for "millet mashed potatoes."

YIELD: SERVES 4

Herbed Brown Rice

This was our all-purpose rice at Cabbagetown. We sauteed the dry rice with onions and garlic for a rich, toasty flavor, then cooked it with herbs. I do this often at home for fun.

2 tablespoons light vegetable oil

2 onions, chopped

2 cloves of garlic, finely chopped

2 cups uncooked brown rice

4 cups water

2 teaspoons dried dill weed or 2 tablespoons finely chopped fresh dill

½ teaspoon dried or finely chopped fresh thyme

½ teaspoon salt

½ teaspoon black pepper

1. In a medium-size pot, heat the oil. Add the onions, garlic, and rice and saute for 5 minutes, stirring frequently.

2. Add the water, herbs, salt, and pepper. Stir so it is all mixed together.

3. Bring to a boil, then reduce the heat and simmer, covered, for about 50 minutes or until the water is absorbed.

4. Let the cooked rice sit in the pot, covered, for 15–20 minutes before serving.

YIELD: SERVES 4–6

Lemon Rice

This yellow Indian rice is hearty and unusual enough to be served by itself with chappatis or parathas, as a main dish along with an Indian soup or salad. Better still, serve it as part of an Indian feast.

2 cups uncooked brown rice
4 cups water
2 teaspoons salt
½ teaspoon turmeric
3–4 whole cloves
10–12 black peppercorns
1 bay leaf
2 tablespoons light vegetable oil
2 tablespoons black mustard seeds
½ teaspoon asafetida
2 fresh hot peppers, finely chopped
3 onions, chopped
1 cup roasted peanuts
2 green peppers, chopped
2 cups fresh or frozen green peas
2 tablespoons ground cumin
1 ½ teaspoons ground coriander
½ teaspoon cayenne
Juice of 1 lemon
1 ½ teaspoons salt
1 teaspoon molasses
½ cup finely chopped scallions
Chopped fresh cilantro (optional)

1. In a medium-size pot, mix the rice, water, salt, turmeric, cloves, peppercorns, and bay leaf. Cover and cook on low heat until all the water is absorbed, about 40 minutes.

2. In a large soup pot, heat the oil. Fry the mustard seeds until they pop. Add the asafetida and fry, stirring quickly.

3. In this order add the hot peppers, onions, peanuts, peppers, and peas. Cook for 10 minutes.

4. Mix in the cumin, coriander, and cayenne.

5. Add the lemon juice, salt, molasses, and scallions.

6. Mix in the rice and stir well.

7. Serve garnished with chopped fresh cilantro, if available.

YIELD: SERVES 6

Toasted-Corn Polenta

Polenta is a traditional Mexican or Italian dish. It seems to have been ignored by Americans until this decade when it has become as popular as it should be. This recipe makes a rich and creamy preparation of cornmeal which marries well with all forms of tomato sauces, beans, and roasted vegetables. Serve Toasted-Corn Polenta alongside beans or topped with the flavorful New Mexico Red Chile Sauce or the Long-Simmered Tomato Sauce, with asparagus, spinach, roasted summer squash, or with a stir-fry.

Leftover polenta can be cut in slices and fried for breakfast or any other meal.

2 cups yellow, blue, or white cornmeal
6–8 cups water
2 teaspoons salt
2 tablespoons olive oil
2 small onions, chopped (optional)
1 cup fresh or frozen corn (optional)
Freshly ground black pepper

1. Heat the dry cornmeal in a heavy pot, stirring constantly until it just starts to brown and turn fragrant. Very slowly add the water, stirring vigorously after each addition, until the cornmeal absorbs the water and is smooth. If the mixture is really thick after adding 6 cups of water, gradually stir in up to 2 more cups of water. (The key to getting the water right for a really creamy polenta is a matter of inspiration and experience.)

continues . . .

2. Add salt and olive oil. Add onion and corn if desired. Continue stirring over medium heat until the mixture begins to shine. Taste and add more salt if necessary.

3. Pour into one or two shallow baking dishes, lightly coated with olive oil. Sprinkle with freshly ground black pepper.

4. Bake in a 350° oven until the cornmeal mixture develops a nice crust, 45–60 minutes. If the top starts to get hard, drizzle it with a bit of olive oil.

5. To serve, cut baked polenta in squares or wedges.

Herbed Polenta

Mix 1 teaspoon fresh thyme or tarragon or any herbs you like into the cornmeal mixture before you bake it.

YIELD: SERVES 6–8

Blended White Basmati Rice

One benefit of being a vegetarian for so long is that I have mellowed and now allow myself to eat and enjoy white rice again.

Grains like quinoa, amaranth, and teff are wonderful but I find them often too bitter to eat alone. After many years of eating them by themselves, I have experimented with mixing them with long grain white rice or white basmati rice. This gives a beautiful balanced, light flavor. I've cooked these grains this way for years and people agree that the combination is wonderful.

1⅓ cup uncooked long grain white or basmati rice

⅔ cup uncooked quinoa, amaranth, teff, or bulghur
   (available at natural foods stores)

4 cups water

Pinch or two of salt

1–2 pats butter (*optional, non-vegan*)

1 tablespoon ume shiso condiment (optional—available in macrobiotic
   sections of natural foods stores)

1. In a medium-size pot, rinse the rice and whichever grain you choose from quinoa, amaranth, teff, or bulghur.

2. In a pot cover the grains with 4 cups water, add a pinch of salt, and bring to a boil.

3. Turn down the heat. Cover and simmer for about 20–25 minutes until the water is absorbed.

4. Let the cooked rice sit for 15 minutes in the pot, covered, to make it fluffier.

5. If you eat butter, melt 1 or 2 pats on top of the grains in the pot—the flavor is amazing. If you don't eat butter, try sprinkling a bit of ume shiso condiment as a garnish.

YIELD: SERVES 4

How to Cook Beans

Bean cooking is my current major art form. Beans are all cooked in a similar way. The deliciousness comes in cooking them long enough, then adding seasonings to enhance the flavor toward the end of the cooking. Here are detailed steps for cooking beans, followed by a recipe for cooked pinto beans which can be used for many of the bean dishes in this cookbook.

1. Sort for stones. There are lots of stones in beans. The easiest way to find them (rather than biting into them and having your teeth break) is to spread the dry beans out on a cookie sheet and work your way from one end of the cookie sheet to the other pulling out all rocks, sticks, or misshapen beans (they often won't absorb water in cooking).

2. Soak the beans overnight. Cover the beans with generous amounts of water. Soak overnight or at least 12 hours. Soaking is actually rehydrating a dried food. The beans will increase dramatically in size.

3. Pour off soaking water. Cover the beans in pot with new water. As you'll notice in my Clay Pot Black Bean recipe (on page 78), I like cooking beans in clay pots. This is traditional and gives the beans a delicious flavor. However, you can cook beans in any cooking pot.

4. Bring the beans and water to a boil uncovered. Boil 10 minutes. Skim off foam. The foam contains a lot of the indigestible sugars from the beans. Without it the beans are much more digestible.

5. Add ½ stick kombu seaweed. This makes a big difference in the softness of the beans and their digestibility. I always use kombu seaweed when cooking beans.

6. Cook covered or partly covered on a low simmer. Large beans cook in about 2 hours. Smaller beans cook anywhere from 1 to 2 hours. However one of the golden rules is that you can't overcook a bean. Longer cooking only makes it more delicious. Sometimes I leave my pot on the woodstove for 6 hours. Be careful—you may need to add more water. (You may want to peek at the beans somewhere in the middle of the cooking process.)

7. Do not add salt until the bean is well cooked and soft. If you add salt too early, the beans will stay hard, no matter how long you cook them. I always use "two salts" to bring out the flavor of the beans: sea salt and tamari, or sea salt and miso.

8. Other seasonings I add to beans after I add the salt are chopped onion and celery, chopped garlic, a tablespoon or two of olive oil, chopped fresh herbs (especially cilantro), and whole or chopped red hot peppers.

9. Continue to cook and taste. A well cooked and well seasoned bean is delicious, so don't stop until your bean gets there.

Cooked & Seasoned Pinto Beans

Cooked Beans (steps 1–6)

   2 cups dry pinto beans

   6 cups cooking water

   ½ stick kombu seaweed

"Two Salts" (step 7)

   1 teaspoon salt

   2 teaspoons tamari

Seasonings for Cooked Pinto Beans (step 8)

   2 onions, diced

   2 stalks celery, sliced

   1 teaspoon dried or fresh thyme

   2 tablespoons olive oil

   1 ancho chile, whole, or seeded and chopped (optional)

Follow the detailed bean cooking instructions.

YIELD: 5–6 CUPS COOKED BEANS

Adzuki Beans with Squash

When the squash ripens in the garden in late summer, try this classic hearty bean dish.

2 cups uncooked adzuki beans

6 cups water

½ stick kombu seaweed

1 medium-size butternut or kabocha squash (2–3 pounds)

1–2 teaspoons tamari

1–1 ½ teaspoons sea salt

2 scallions, chopped

1. Sort through the beans for stones. Adzuki beans, contrary to the rule for most beans, do not need soaking. Rinse the adzuki beans thoroughly. In a large pot, cover the adzuki beans with water. Add the kombu. Bring to a boil, uncovered, for 10 minutes. Skim foam from the beans. Turn down to a simmer. Partially cover pot, and cook for 1 hour on low heat until beans are soft.

2. Dice the butternut or kabocha squash into 1-inch cubes (you don't have to peel homegrown butternut or kabocha squash—the cooked skin is totally fine and edible). Add the squash to the top of the beans in the pot. Add enough water to keep the beans from burning. Cover and continue cooking on low heat for another 25–30 minutes.

3. When the squash is tender, stir it into the beans. Add tamari and sea salt to taste.

4. Transfer to a serving bowl. Garnish with chopped scallions.

YIELD: SERVES 4–6

Red Chile Chick Peas

There are many varieties of dried red chile peppers grown and widely available today. Whole chiles cooked with chick peas give the beans some hotness, but mostly a rich smokey flavor. Try different types of chiles. Some variety names may be New Mexico, ancho, or pasilla. (By the way, chick peas cooked with red chiles make a delightful hummus). A simple grain and roasted vegetables are good accompaniments for Red Chile Chick Peas.

> 2 cups uncooked chick peas (garbanzos)
>
> 6 cups water for cooking
>
> ½ stick kombu seaweed
>
> 2 dried New Mexico red chile peppers
>
> 2 tablespoons olive oil
>
> ½ teaspoon freshly ground black pepper
>
> 1 heaping teaspoon salt

1. Sort the chick peas for stones. Rinse. Place in a large pot and cover with water. Let stand soaking at least 12 hours. Drain.

2. Cover generously with fresh water. Heat to boiling. Boil uncovered 10 minutes and skim off the foam. (This step makes beans more digestible.)

3. Add the kombu. Reduce heat, partly cover, and cook over medium heat until soft, about 2 hours.

4. Add the chiles. (Leave the seeds in for hot chick peas; remove the seeds for a milder dish.)

5. Add the olive oil, pepper, and salt. Always wait until beans are soft before adding salt. If you add salt too early, the beans will stay hard, no matter how long you cook them.

6. Cook and cook, covered, at least one hour more. Add more water, if necessary.

7. The dish is ready when the chick peas are very soft and have a delicious rich flavor. Try to cook off most of the liquid, so the beans are in a thick broth.

8. Serve warm or at room temperature.

YIELD: SERVES 4–6

Clay Pot Black Beans with Cilantro

Black beans are always good. Serve these black beans with a simple grain or polenta and blanched vegetables with my fresh Lemon & Garlic Dressing (page 47). Mitlas are an heirloom variety of black beans, especially richly flavored. I learned to cook mitlas in New Mexico in an Apache clay pot, then finish them off with fresh cilantro. Of course you can cook beans in any pot.

2 cups uncooked black turtle beans or mitlas

6 cups water

½ stick kombu

2 medium onions, chopped (about 1 cup)

2 tablespoons olive oil

1 tablespoon ground cumin

1 teaspoon salt

¼ teaspoon freshly ground black pepper

½ cup chopped fresh cilantro

1. Wash and sort the beans for stones. Place in large pot (clay pot or otherwise). Cover with water. Soak for at least 12 hours. Drain.

2. Cover generously with fresh water. Heat to boiling. Boil uncovered 10 minutes; skim off the foam.

3. Add kombu. Reduce heat, cover, and cook over low heat until soft, about 2 hours.

4. Add chopped onions, olive oil, cumin, salt, and pepper.

5. Cook at least 1 hour more. Add more water, if necessary. The beans should be very soft, melting, rich, and succulent. If they aren't, cook longer.

6. Add cilantro and cook a few minutes longer.

7. Taste and correct seasonings.

YIELD: SERVES 4–6

Entrees

One of the major misconceptions about vegetarian cooking is that you won't be filled up after a meal—that somehow something is missing. With this collection of entrees that myth should be dispelled. There is something for everyone, and many of the dishes included here—such as lasagne, pasta, or quiche—will be familiar to many. Some of the recipes such as quiche or lasagne have a number of steps and components involved in their preparation. I make them when I have time and want a special meal.

Pasta—almost everyone's favorite. In this chapter are detailed instructions for cooking pasta, as well as for pasta sauces and entrees featuring pasta.

Ethnic dishes have become major inspirations for vegetarians. Rice and beans should be served with Mexican entrees. Choose Chile Rellenos, Burritos, traditional New Mexico Layered Red Chile Enchiladas, or the Cabbagetown del Dia Enchiladas— where it's your choice from the recipes for many tempting vegetable fillings.

Indian cooking is traditionally vegetarian, so it offers many dishes to choose from. Curries should be accompanied by dal (see Cabbage Dal) and rice (see Blended White Basmati Rice or Lemon Rice). Other Indian specialties in this book are the Pakoras, Parathas, Indian Lentil Soup, Indian Spinach & Peanut Soup, Koshimbir, and Cucumber Raita. A sample Indian-style dinner might include Dry Potato Curry, Cabbage Dal, Cucumber Raita, and Parathas.

Season's Stir-Fry

My stir-fry technique is really a "steam-frying." I use oil and water, so vegetables stay flavorful and crisp, and light rather than oily. I add tofu to the vegetables, season them with garlic, ginger, and tamari, soy sauce, or the Chinese Master Sauce. I serve the stir-fry over plain brown rice or Herbed Brown Rice. A stir-fry is what you're looking for when you want a light, hot, and nutritious meal. You can vary it by using any vegetables that are in season.

From working in a restaurant kitchen I've developed a certain meticulousness in cooking, most obvious to me when I make stir-fries at home. I like to have the counter very clean, the vegetables very clean, and I like to put each vegetable in a separate little container as I cut it for the stir-fry. This is the way we do it in a restaurant. We're careful with the preparation, so when it comes time to cook the stir-fry, there is a feeling of order and care which makes cooking feel good.

4 cups cooked brown rice (page 65) or Herbed Brown Rice (page 69)
2 cups Baked Herbed Tofu (page 51)
2 stalks broccoli, cut in bite-size pieces (6 cups)
4 cloves of garlic, finely chopped
½-inch piece fresh ginger, finely chopped
2 tablespoons dark sesame oil or Chinese Master Sauce (page 82)
2 tablespoons light vegetable oil
2 carrots, sliced
2 celery stalks, sliced
2 onions, cut in crescents
1 wedge green cabbage, coarsely sliced (2 cups)
2 tablespoons tamari, soy sauce, or Chinese Master Sauce (page 82)
Fresh lemon juice (optional)

1. First prepare the rice and the tofu.

2. Steam or blanch the broccoli for about 5 minutes until it's just tender when pierced with a knife. Remove to a bowl and set aside.

3. To prepare the seasoning mixture, chop the garlic and ginger together. Put it in a small bowl, and cover it with 2 tablespoons dark sesame oil or Chinese Master Sauce.

4. It takes 15–20 minutes to cook a stir-fry, and you want to serve it immediately after you finish cooking it, so time your cooking accordingly.

When you are ready to begin (all the vegetables are ready), heat 2 tablespoons light vegetable oil in a large frying pan or wok. Toss in the carrots and cook for 2 minutes, stirring occasionally with a wooden spoon or wok spatula. Add ½ cup of water and steam-fry the carrots about 3 minutes more, or until most of the water is gone and the carrots are just starting to become tender. Add the celery and cook for about 3 minutes, until the celery just starts to become tender.

5. Add the onions, then the garlic-ginger-sesame oil mixture or enough Master Sauce to moisten. Cook and stir until the onions just start to become limp, about 2 minutes. Add more water if necessary to keep the vegetables from sticking.

6. Add the broccoli and Herbed Baked Tofu, and cook until warm, 2–3 minutes. Add more water if necessary.

7. Stir in 2 tablespoons more tamari or Master Sauce, and immediately add the cabbage. Stir well. Add 1–2 tablespoons more water, and continue cooking until the cabbage is hot, about 5 minutes. The mixture should look colorful and fresh, tender and juicy. That's the balance you're striving for. Taste. You might want to add a little fresh lemon juice to sharpen the flavors.

8. Spoon 1 cup hot rice onto individual serving plates and top with a mound of hot vegetables. Chopsticks work better than forks with stir-fries. Also put tamari or soy sauce and the pepper grinder on the table.

Spring Stir-Fry

Steam asparagus instead of the broccoli. Add snow peas and fresh spinach leaves instead of the cabbage.

Summer Stir-Fry

Steam green beans along with the broccoli. Add sliced zucchini instead of celery. Add finely chopped fresh green herbs to the seasoning mixture.

Autumn Stir-Fry

You can change the character of the stir-fry by adding sliced fresh tomatoes. Add them right after the onions and cook so they juice up. Add fresh corn kernels after the tomatoes.

continues . . .

Winter Stir-Fry

Slice parsnips, potatoes, or sweet potatoes, and add them along with the carrots. Fry 2 cups sliced mushrooms separately in oil at high heat, until golden brown. Add along with the broccoli and tofu.

Vegan Option:

If using Chinese Master Sauce (steps 3, 7), make it with rice syrup instead of honey.

YIELD: SERVES 4

Chinese Master Sauce

This is a spicy Oriental sauce, with ginger, cinnamon, and star anise. Marinate vegetables in it before you stir-fry them, or soak dried mushrooms and bean threads in it. Use master sauce as liquid in your pan while you're making Season's Stir-Fry. Or heat up the sauce and pour it over a cooked stir-fry instead of using tamari or soy sauce. Tasty cooked carrots, a by-product of making this sauce, can be eaten as a vegetable snack.

½ cup tamari sauce

1 tablespoon honey OR rice syrup (*vegan option*)

½ cup water

2 teaspoons dark sesame oil

2 cloves star anise

1 clove garlic, mashed

2 slices fresh ginger root, minced

½ stick cinnamon

1 or 2 scallions, minced

2 carrots, sliced

1. Mix all the ingredients together in a small saucepan and simmer for 25–30 minutes.

2. Strain the simmered sauce. Keep Chinese Master Sauce in a jar in the refrigerator until you want to use it.

YIELD: 1 1/2 CUPS

Scrambled Tofu

I invented this tofu dish for brunch customers who don't eat eggs, but it caught on with everyone. You cook tofu and vegetables separately, mix them all together, and then fry them up with extra dark sesame oil and tamari. This dish is good for dinner as well as brunch. Serve it with a thick slice of whole wheat bread or sourdough.

4 cups Herbed Baked Tofu (double the recipe on page 51)

4 potatoes

1 stalk broccoli, cut in bite-size pieces (2–3 cups)

1 tablespoon light vegetable oil

3 carrots, sliced

1 teaspoon dried marjoram or 1 tablespoon finely chopped fresh marjoram

1 tablespoon light vegetable oil

2 onions, cut in crescents

2 cloves of garlic, finely chopped

1 teaspoon dried or finely chopped fresh tarragon

½ teaspoon dried or finely chopped fresh thyme

2 cups fresh or frozen green peas or corn

1 tablespoon light vegetable oil

1 tablespoon dark sesame oil

1 tablespoon tamari or soy sauce

Tamari-Roasted Almonds (page 3)

1. First prepare the tofu. Put in a large bowl.

2. Scrub the potatoes well but do not peel. Cook in water to cover until tender, about 30 minutes after the water boils. Dice into bite-size cubes. Add to the tofu in the bowl.

3. Steam or blanch the broccoli for about 5 minutes, until just tender. Add to the bowl.

4. In a medium-size frying pan, heat 1 tablespoon oil. Add the carrots and saute for about 3 minutes, then add ¼ cup of water to steam until the carrots are tender and the water is absorbed. This takes about 5 minutes more. Stir in the marjoram. Add to the vegetables in the bowl.

continues . . .

5. In the same frying pan, heat another 1 tablespoon oil. Add the onions and garlic and saute until limp, 3–4 minutes. Add the tarragon, thyme, and peas or corn. Saute for 2–3 minutes to thaw the frozen vegetables or to cook the fresh ones very lightly. Remove to the bowl.

6. At this stage you can cover the mixture and refrigerate until ready to serve, or you can fry it up right away. Heat 1 tablespoon vegetable oil in a frying pan. Add the tofu-vegetable mixture from the bowl. Cook until hot, stirring frequently. When hot, stir in 1 tablespoon dark sesame oil and 1 tablespoon tamari or soy sauce. Taste and adjust the seasonings.

7. Serve immediately, sprinkled with almonds.

Vegetable Scrambled Tofu

You can add many other vegetables. I like steamed cauliflower, steamed green beans, lightly sauteed zucchini, and sauteed mushrooms.

YIELD: SERVES 4

uiche

Here is a basic recipe for quiche, a rich vegetable, egg, and cheese custard in a whole wheat crust. A tofu variation follows.

One 9-inch or 10-inch Whole Wheat Pie Crust (page 87)

3 tablespoons butter

1 onion, cut in crescents

2 cups chopped vegetables

Herbs (I especially like thyme, tarragon, and dill.)

Freshly ground black pepper

3 eggs

¼ teaspoon salt

1 ½ cups combination milk and heavy cream
    (The more cream you use, the richer your quiche will be.)

Pinch nutmeg or mustard powder

2 cups grated cheese or mixture of cheeses

1. First roll out the pie crust.

2. Prepare the vegetables. In a medium-size frying pan, melt the butter. Add the onion and saute for 2–3 minutes, until it just starts to get limp. Then add the vegetables you're featuring in the quiche and cook until quite tender. (You want the vegetables in a quiche to be well cooked to bring out the deep and rich aspects of their flavor.) Add herbs and freshly ground black pepper to taste.

3. Next make the custard. In a medium-size bowl, beat the eggs with a whisk. Whisk in the salt, then the milk and heavy cream, then the nutmeg or mustard.

4. To assemble the quiche, sprinkle half the cheese in the pie crust. Spread the vegetables over the cheese. Do not pack the vegetables over the cheese. Do not pack the vegetables tightly. The custard should get inside the vegetable layer and puff it up to make a light and delicate quiche. Sprinkle with the remaining cheese. Pour in as much custard as your pie crust will hold. If you have any custard left over, store it in the refrigerator. It will keep well for 2 days, and you can use it in an omelet or scrambled eggs or another quiche.

5. Bake in a preheated 350° oven for about 40 minutes, or until the quiche is lightly browned and the custard is firm in the center.

6. Allow to settle for 20 minutes before serving so the texture can firm and the quiche can cool to its best flavor.

Spinach Feta Quiche

Saute onion with garlic and 6 ounces fresh spinach. Season with basil and thyme. Add crumbled feta to the cheese mixture.

Blushing Tomato Quiche

Saute onions with 3 sliced fresh ripe tomatoes and 2 tablespoons capers. Season with thyme, tarragon, or dill.

continues . . .

Tofu Quiche

I like broccoli about the best in tofu quiche.

> **One 9-inch or 10-inch Vegan Whole Wheat Pie Crust (page 88)**
>
> 3 tablespoons olive oil
>
> 1 onion, cut in crescents
>
> 2 cups chopped vegetables
>
> ½ cup chopped black olives (optional)
>
> 2 tablespoons chopped herbs (Fresh herbs are best.)
>
> Freshly ground black pepper
>
> 1 pound tofu
>
> Juice of ½ lemon
>
> 2 teaspoons tamari
>
> ½–1 teaspoon salt

1. First roll out the pie crust.

2. Prepare the vegetables. In a medium-size frying pan, heat the oil. Add the onion and saute for 2–3 minutes, until it just starts to get limp. Then add the vegetables you're featuring and cook until quite tender. (You want the vegetables in a quiche to be well cooked to bring out the deep and rich aspects of their flavor.) Add olives, herbs, and freshly ground black pepper to taste. Set aside.

3. Crumble or blend tofu with juice of ½ lemon, tamari, and salt and more pepper to taste. In a bowl, mix seasoned vegetables into the tofu mixture. (Don't layer the tofu and veggies.)

4. Pour the vegetable-tofu mixture into the prepared pie crust.

5. Bake in preheated 350° oven for approximately 40 minutes.

YIELD: ONE 9- OR 10-INCH QUICHE.

SERVES 4–6

Whole Wheat Pie Crusts

These are for quiches and pies. They are very tender but you must use whole wheat pastry flour or a combination of pastry flour and oat flour. Don't try making these with bread flour. If at all possible, use freshly ground flour. A vegan whole wheat pie crust, using corn oil instead of butter, is given as a variation.

I always make 2 crusts at a time. If it's worth making 1, it's worth making 2. You can store the extra crust in a plastic bag in the freezer, and it's ready for an instant quiche or fruit pie.

Note that not all pie pans are created equal. The recipes for pie crusts and quiche and dessert pie fillings are best in deep-dish glass or ceramic pie pans (not flimsy aluminum ones!).

2½ cups whole wheat pastry flour
(or part whole wheat pastry flour and part oat flour)
¼ teaspoon salt
¾ cup cold butter
About ½ cup cold water or milk

1. In a mixing bowl, mix together the flour and salt with a fork. Grate the cold butter with a medium grater over the flour. Toss with a fork until the butter is evenly distributed.

2. Toss in the cold water or milk a little at a time and stir lightly with the fork. The exact amount of liquid will vary with the properties of the flour you are using, the temperature of the butter, how hot and humid the weather is, and the way you like your dough to feel when you roll it out. You have added enough liquid when you can press the dough with your hands and it holds together. The mixture will still look pretty loose and dry. It should not be wet or sticky.

3. Form the dough into 2 balls.

4. Butter two 9-inch or 10-inch pie pans well to prevent sticking.

5. Now roll out the crusts, 1 at a time. First knead the ball about 10 times on a floured counter so the ball holds together. To get it into the best shape for rolling, first press the dough down so it becomes a flattened ball. Then push it down in the center to make a medium-size dent. Last, turn the dough around on the counter, pressing the edges with cupped palms so the whole edge becomes smooth.

continues . . .

6. Lift up the dough and lightly flour the whole counter. With a lightly floured rolling pin, roll the dough, starting from the center and rolling outward. Turn the dough over frequently as you roll so it doesn't stick. Continue flouring the rolling pin and counter as needed.

7. Roll the crust until it shows about 1 inch around the top on an inverted pie pan. Fold the crust in half, and lift it into the pan. Unfold it, and ease it down so it fits smoothly. Fold under the edges of the crust, then flute the rim. If you haven't fluted a crust before, ask a friend to show you. It's satisfying to do and beautiful to look at.

8. Prick the crust with fork and store it in a plastic bag in the refrigerator for a short time or the freezer for a longer time, until you're ready to use it.

Vegan Whole Wheat Pie Crusts

These are more difficult to handle and roll out than pie crusts made with butter, but are *very* tasty.

> **2 ⅓ cups whole wheat pastry flour (or part whole wheat pastry flour and part oat flour)**
> **¼ teaspoon salt**
> **½ cup corn oil**
> **½ cup water**

1. Whisk oil and water together until droplets of oil are suspended in the water.

2. In a medium-size bowl, mix together the flour and salt. Toss the liquid gently into the flour until the mixture is moist enough to hold together. This pie crust dough will be a little wetter than the butter crust. The dough should be moist enough to be formed into a ball but not be too damp. The crust won't be flaky (you need butter for flakiness) but it will be tender and light.

3. Form the dough into 2 balls.

4. Oil two 9-inch or 10-inch pie pans well to prevent sticking.

5. Roll out the crust, 1 at a time—following steps 5–8 in the recipe (with butter) as above.

YIELD: TWO 9- OR IO-INCH PIE CRUSTS

How to Cook Pasta

The crucial skill in cooking pasta is to cook it just until a fine core of firmness remains at the center of each strand—that is, pasta cooked "*al dente.*" Pasta cooked correctly is a different food, flavorful, exciting, and substantial.

Try tasting the pasta as it cooks. When a strand is dry, starchy, rigid in the center it's not cooked enough. But if the pasta is soft all the way through you've cooked it too long. You can't test the pasta's doneness this way with fresh pasta, since it has no core, which is why I prefer dried pasta.

The following method can be used for all pasta—for salads, casseroles, tossed pasta dishes, and pasta with sauce. One pound of pasta serves 4 people.

1 teaspoon dried basil (optional)

½ teaspoon dried whole rosemary, slightly crushed in your hands (optional)

1 pound pasta

2 tablespoons unsalted butter, OR olive oil (*vegan option*)

Fresh lemon juice

1. Fill a soup pot or any large pot about ⅔ full of water. Bring to a boil. If desired, add the basil and rosemary to the pasta cooking water as it comes to a boil. (Use this option only for Italian or continental-style dishes.)

2. Add the pasta. Return to a rolling boil, stir once, and continue to cook uncovered at a rolling boil.

3. Taste the pasta as it cooks. The amount of time to cook pasta *al dente* is very different depending on which pasta you're cooking (it will be approximately the same as or slightly less than that recommended on the instructions on the pasta box). Stir once or twice to keep it from sticking to the bottom of the pot. The surest way to tell if pasta is done is to take out a piece and bite it. It's done when it's cooked through except for a tiny hard center.

4. Pour the pasta into a colander to drain it, but do not rinse. A bit of stickiness is part of the charm of pasta.

5. Return the pasta to the cooking pot and toss in 2 tablespoons butter or olive oil. The butter or olive oil enriches the flavor and keeps the strands separate. Add a few squeezes of fresh lemon juice, and maybe a little salt. The pasta is now ready to use. Try this pasta recipe with Fresh Tomato Sauce (page 90). More pasta dishes are given in the following recipes (pages 91-95).

YIELD: SERVES 4

"Fresh Tomato Sauce

When you have good pasta and want to show it off in style, this simple sauce is what you're looking for. I love to serve it sprinkled generously with parmesan cheese.

3 tablespoons olive oil

1 onion, chopped

4 cloves of garlic, finely chopped

Freshly ground black pepper

1 teaspoon dried or finely chopped fresh oregano

1 quart canned tomatoes or 6–8 fresh ripe tomatoes, chopped

Salt to taste

1. In a medium-size frying pan, heat the olive oil. Add the onion and garlic and saute until tender, about 3 minutes. Add the pepper and oregano and cook 1 minute more, stirring constantly.

2. Add the canned or fresh tomatoes and simmer for about 15 minutes, until the sauce starts to thicken. Add salt to taste. Canned tomatoes usually have enough salt, but you might want to add ½–1 teaspoon salt to a fresh tomato sauce.

3. Keep the sauce warm until you're ready to serve it over freshly cooked pasta.

YIELD: 2 ½ CUPS.

SERVES 4-6

Pasta with Garlic & Hot Peppers

I live on this dish and its variations.

3 bulbs garlic (18–24 cloves)

½ cup olive oil

2–3 dried chipotle peppers or any other dried hot peppers you like

1 pound pasta

Balsamic vinegar

Sea salt

Freshly ground black pepper

Freshly grated parmesan cheese (*optional, non-vegan*)

1. Peel the garlic and cut each clove into about 3 chunks.

2. Start the olive oil heating in a small pot. Add garlic and add enough additional olive oil to cover. Cook over very low heat for about 15 minutes.

3. Judge how many peppers you want to use by how hot you like food. Cut peppers into smallish pieces. Add to the garlic and olive oil. Cook about 15 minutes more, until the garlic is browning and sweet.

4. Cook pasta *al dente* (How to Cook Pasta, page 89).

5. Toss the cooked pasta with as much of the garlic, pepper, and olive oil mixture as your pasta absorbs quickly without getting oily. (Pastas are different; the exact amount of oil mixture needed will depend on the pasta.) Taste to be sure it's nicely flavored—too little and the pasta is bland; too much makes it too rich and oily. Save any extra oil mixture in the refrigerator.

6. Serve into individual pasta bowls. Sprinkle each serving with a tiny bit of balsamic vinegar, salt, freshly ground black pepper, and plenty of fresh-grated parmesan cheese, if desired.

Tomato & Kale Variations

• Add 4–6 chopped fresh or canned tomatoes to the garlic, hot peppers, and olive oil at the end of step 3. Cook a short time more. Proceed to the next variation or step 4.

• To the above mixture add 2 cups freshly blanched kale. Cook a minute or two longer. Proceed to step 4.

YIELD: SERVES 4

Pad Thai

Today's favorite food. It doesn't taste quite the same at home as it does in a Thai restaurant, but it's close. If you can't find traditional Thai rice-stick noodles, substitute linguine. You can make peanut sauce ahead of time and keep it in your refrigerator. The pasta can also be cooked ahead of time.

Peanut Sauce (steps 1–6)

3 cloves garlic

½-inch piece ginger root, peeled and minced

2 tablespoons peanut oil

1 teaspoon red pepper flakes

¼ cup tamari

¾ cup water

¾ cup peanut butter

3 tablespoons honey OR rice syrup (*vegan option*)

Pasta: Select *either* rice-stick noodles or linguine. (step 7)

1 pound Thai rice-stick noodles (Soak in a large bowl or warm water for at least 20–30 minutes or until they are soft. Drain before using.)

1 pound linguine (Cook according to How to Cook Pasta, page 89.)

Tofu & Vegetables (steps 8–14)

2 tablespoon peanut oil

1 pound tofu, cut into matchstick-size pieces

¼ cup scallions, chopped

4 tablespoons lime juice

1 pound mung bean sprouts

Garnishes (step 15)

½ cup roasted peanuts, chopped

½ cup fresh cilantro, chopped

1 lime, cut in wedges

1. Mince the garlic. Grate or mince finely the ginger root (you should get about 1 rounded teaspoon of grated ginger).

2. Heat 2 tablespoons of the peanut oil in a medium saucepan over medium heat.

3. Saute garlic and ginger until lightly brown.

4. Add the pepper flakes and then the tamari and water. Heat to a simmer.

5. Stir in the peanut butter and honey or rice syrup, mixing well. The consistency should be thick but pourable.

6. Add more water slowly if it is too thick. Remove the peanut sauce from heat and put aside.

7. If using rice noodles and they are soft, drain at this time. If using linguine, cook according to How to Cook Pasta, page 89.

8. Arrange all the ingredients in an range accessible range from your wok or sauteeing pan.

9. Set a wok or sauteeing pan over medium heat.

10. When the wok or pan is hot, add the other 2 tablespoons of the peanut oil. Make sure oil coats the wok.

11. When the oil is hot, add the tofu and scallions and stir-fry for 1–2 minutes.

12. Add the drained, soaked rice noodles or the cooked linguine, tossing the noodles to coat with the oil.

13. Add 1 cup of the peanut sauce to the noodles, stirring constantly. If texture is too thick, add additional warm water, 1 tablespoon at a time.

14. Add the lime juice and mung bean sprouts.

15. Remove from heat and serve warm garnished with chopped peanuts, cilantro, and wedges of lime.

YIELD: SERVES 6

Basil Pesto on "Bow-Ties"

It's a great moment every year when the scent of fresh-picked basil fills the kitchen and I make pesto.

Basil Pesto (steps 1–3)

Big bunch of basil (3 cups leaves and tender stems)

¾ cup pine nuts or walnuts

2–3 garlic cloves, peeled

1 teaspoon salt (or ½ teaspoon salt plus 1 tablespoon miso or ½ teaspoon salt plus 2 teaspoons umeboshi paste or umeboshi vinegar)

⅓ cup olive oil

Pasta & Other Ingredients (steps 4–6)

1 pound bow-tie pasta or linguine

Lemon juice (optional)

Freshly grated parmesan cheese (*optional, non-vegan*)

Freshly ground black pepper

1. Get that basil ready! Use all the leaves and the tender parts of the stems near the top.

2. Toast pine nuts in a small skillet over low heat or in the oven. Be very careful as they brown in a matter of minutes.

3. Pulse garlic and basil in a food processor. Add the toasted nuts and salt or salt mixture. Pulse until blended. Add olive oil and pulse just until combined. Your basil pesto is now made.

4. Cook pasta and drain (How to Cook Pasta, page 89).

5. Toss the hot pasta with the basil pesto mixture. Taste. Often a squeeze of fresh lemon juice makes all the flavors zing out.

6. Serve with plenty of fresh parmesan cheese and freshly ground black pepper over each serving.

Pesto Pasta with New Potatoes

A shockingly delicious traditional Italian dish is made by tossing ½ pound cooked halved new potatoes with the cooked pasta and pesto. I particularly enjoy the small purple Peruvian potatoes.

YIELD: SERVES 4

Mom's Macaroni & Cheese

My mom made this elegant mac and cheese for us kids. Be sure to use soft bread. Dry bread crumbs soak up the custard and ruin the dish.

¾ cup uncooked whole wheat macaroni

¾ cup soft bread crumbs (fresh, crumbled)

2 tablespoons butter

½ pound cheddar cheese, grated (about 2 cups)

1 ¼ cups hot milk

1 small onion, finely chopped

¼ cup finely chopped fresh parsley

½ teaspoon salt

2 eggs, beaten

1. Cook the macaroni in boiling water according to the instructions in How to Cook Pasta (page 89).

2. In a large bowl, combine the bread crumbs, butter, and cheese. Pour in the hot milk. Add the onion, parsley, and salt. At this point, taste. If the sauce is not flavorful or cheesy enough, add whatever you feel is lacking.

3. Add the beaten eggs, then the cooked macaroni.

4. Pour into a well-buttered medium-size baking dish.

5. Bake in a preheated 350° oven for about 30 minutes, until the casserole is firm and golden brown.

6. For best flavor, allow to sit for 10 minutes before serving.

YIELD: SERVES 2 HUNGRY PEOPLE OR

4 NOT-SO-HUNGRY ONES

Spinach Lasagne

Lasagne is a favorite entree everywhere I've cooked. It's a classic dish and people unfamiliar with vegetarian food are happy and comfortable with lasagne. Lasagne is a great dish to serve to company since the flavors and textures are actually better if you make it up and bake it in advance, then heat it up just before serving.

> 1½–2 quarts Long-Simmered Tomato Sauce (page 99)
>
> 2 tablespoons olive oil
>
> 8–10 ounces fresh spinach, finely chopped (6 cups)
>
> ½ teaspoon salt
>
> Freshly ground black pepper
>
> 15–16 ounces ricotta cheese (about 2 cups)
>
> 1 egg
>
> Pinch nutmeg
>
> 1 teaspoon finely chopped fresh mint (optional)
>
> ½–¾ pound whole wheat lasagne noodles
>
> 1 pound mozzarella cheese, thinly sliced
>
> 2 cups freshly grated parmesan, romano, or sharp provolone cheese

1. First prepare the sauce.

2. To make the filling, heat the 2 tablespoons olive oil in a medium-size frying pan. Add the spinach and saute until lightly cooked. Season with salt and pepper. In a mixing bowl, combine the ricotta with the egg, nutmeg, and mint. Add the spinach and mix well.

3. Assemble the lasagne in a medium-size (3 quart or larger) baking dish. First, spread olive oil over the bottom of the dish to keep the casserole from sticking. Cover with a thin layer of lasagne sauce. Arrange a single layer of uncooked lasagne noodles over the sauce. Cover with half the ricotta mixture. Smooth it out. Cover with half the sliced mozzarella. Pat it down. Sprinkle with parmesan cheese. Cover with another layer of sauce. Repeat the layers of noodles, the remaining ricotta mixture, the remaining mozzarella, and more parmesan. Spread with another layer of sauce. Cover with a final layer of noodles. Use the remaining sauce as a thick layer on top.

4. Cover the casserole dish. Do not use aluminum foil, since the tomato sauce will eat through it. Bake in a preheated 350° oven for 1 hour to cook the noodles. Then sprinkle with more parmesan cheese. Cover and return to the oven and bake 15–20 minutes. Turn off the heat and allow the lasagne to sit in the oven for 30–60 minutes to firm the textures and let the flavors ripen. Delicious!

5. Serve with a big salad and a good red wine.

Eggplant Parmigiane Lasagne

Slice 1 eggplant in thin slices. Dredge each slice with a coating of whole wheat flour, crushed rosemary, salt, and freshly ground black pepper. Fry the slices in olive oil. Put eggplant layers somewhere in the middle of the lasagne in step 3, and bake as directed above.

Tofu Lasagne

    1 ½–2 quarts Long-Simmered Tomato Sauce (page 99)

    2 tablespoons olive oil

    2 pounds tofu

    4–6 cloves garlic, finely chopped

    ½ teaspoon salt

    Freshly ground black pepper

    1 teaspoon finely chopped fresh mint (optional)

    2 tablespoons olive oil

    16 ounces spinach, finely chopped (10 cups)

1. First prepare the sauce.

2. To make the filling, cut the tofu into slices about ¼-inch thick. In a medium-size frying pan, heat 2 tablespoons olive oil and garlic. Add the tofu and fry until lightly golden on both sides. Season with salt, pepper, and mint. Put aside.

3. Heat another 2 tablespoons olive oil in the frying pan. Then add the spinach, and saute until lightly cooked. Add more salt and pepper to taste if desired. Put aside.

continues . . .

4. Assemble the lasagne in a medium-size baking dish (3-4 quart or larger—try a 9-inch by 13-inch by 3-inch deep covered baking dish). First, spread olive oil over the bottom of the dish to keep the casserole from sticking. Cover with a thin layer (no more than 1/5) of lasagne sauce. Arrange a single layer of uncooked lasagne noodles over the sauce. Then layer half of the tofu and half the spinach. Cover with another sauce layer (¼ of the remaining sauce). Add another layer of noodles, the remaining tofu, the remaining spinach, more sauce (⅓ of the remaining sauce), a final layer of noodles. Finally pour the remaining sauce on top, making sure all the noodles are covered (if not, they will burn).

5. Cover the casserole dish. It is preferable that your baking dish has a glass or ceramic cover. Do not use aluminum foil. Bake in a preheated 350° oven for 46–60 minutes to cook the noodles. Turn off the heat and allow the lasagne to sit in the oven for 30–60 minutes to firm the textures and let the flavors ripen. Delicious!

6. Serve with a big salad. This lasagne is often better reheated and served the second day.

YIELD: SERVES 6–8

Long-Simmered Tomato Sauce

This flavorful sauce has the right juiciness for lasagne. It also is good on cooked pasta.

> 2 quarts canned tomatoes or 12–14 fresh ripe tomatoes, chopped
>
> 2 bay leaves
>
> 2 onions, diced
>
> 6–8 cloves of garlic, finely chopped
>
> 1 ½ teaspoons fennel seeds
>
> 2 teaspoons dried basil or 2 tablespoons finely chopped fresh basil
>
> 1 teaspoon dried or finely chopped fresh oregano
>
> 2 teaspoons dried or finely chopped fresh thyme
>
> 1 teaspoon dried or fresh whole rosemary, finely chopped
>
> Freshly ground black pepper
>
> Salt to taste

1. In a large pot, cook the tomatoes with the bay leaves, onions, and garlic. Simmer gently, uncovered for about 1 hour, stirring frequently to keep the tomatoes from sticking.

2. Add the herbs and pepper. Continue to simmer for 30 minutes to blend the flavors. At the restaurant we called this "letting the ingredients get to know each other."

3. Taste and reseason. Canned tomatoes usually have enough salt, but if you're using fresh tomatoes, you might want to add about 1 teaspoon salt. If the sauce is bitter, add more thyme or more black pepper, both of which help sweeten tomatoes.

YIELD: 1 ½–2 QUARTS.

ENOUGH FOR 1 RECIPE OF SPINACH LASAGNE

Enchiladas del Dia

At Cabbagetown Café this was our best-selling entree. We made a different enchilada filling every day, hence the "del dia." Fillings varied from simple classics like raw onions with fresh herbs and sour cream, to seasonal steamed asparagus with lemon and pepper, to our favorite spicy corn, green pepper, almond, and cheese filling. I recommend that you serve refried beans and rice on the plate with the enchiladas. I sometimes enjoy a very light cole slaw made with red cabbage, my Fresh Lemon & Garlic Dressing (page 47), and chopped cilantro as a side salad on enchilada plates

> 2 cups Refried Beans (page 2)
>
> 2 cups Herbed Brown Rice (page 69)
>
> 2 cups Cabbagetown Enchilada Sauce (page 105) or
>   New Mexico Red Chile Sauce (page 107)
>
> 2 cups enchilada filling of your choice (pages 101–104)
>
> 2 tablespoons butter, OR corn oil (*vegan option*) to fry tortillas
>
> 4 corn tortillas
>
> 2–4 cups grated monterey jack or cheddar cheese (*optional, non-vegan*)

1. First make the refried beans, herbed rice, and sauce.

2. Choose the enchilada filling you want from the recipes on the following pages. Prepare the filling.

3. In a medium-size frying pan, melt the butter or heat the oil. Soft-fry each corn tortilla in the butter by cooking it on one side until it starts to get limp, then turn it over and fry it for a second or two more until it's all soft. Roll ½ cup of filling inside each tortilla. Store the filled tortillas on a plate covered with a plastic bag in the refrigerator until you're ready to serve dinner.

4. On each ovenproof enchilada plate, put 1 rolled enchilada. Cover with about ½ cup sauce, being especially careful to cover the ends of the enchilada so they don't dry out during baking. Arrange ½ cup herbed rice and ½ cup refried beans next to each enchilada on the plate. Sprinkle it all with 1 cup of grated cheese. Or put all 4 enchiladas in a medium-size baking dish, cover with sauce, and sprinkle with 2 cups of grated cheese.

5. Bake in a preheated 350° oven for 15–20 minutes, until the cheese is melted and bubbly around the edges.

6. Serve immediately. A dollop of sour cream or guacamole and a few black olives are excellent additions to each plate.

YIELD: 4 ENCHILADAS. SERVES 4

The Original Cabbagetown Enchilada Filling

Here is the original Cabbagetown enchilada. It's full of corn, green peppers, almonds, and cheese, and is very nicely spiced.

½ cup almonds

3 tablespoons olive oil

2 green peppers, diced

2 cups fresh or frozen corn

1 teaspoon ground cumin

½ teaspoon ground coriander

¼ teaspoon cayenne

1 cup grated cheddar cheese

1. Toast the almonds in a 350° oven or toaster oven for about 20 minutes, or until lightly browned. Chop in half.

2. Heat the oil in a frying pan. Add the green peppers and saute over high heat until they are blistered and tender, about 3 minutes. Add the corn and cook for 2–3 minutes more. Add the spices and saute for 1 minute, stirring constantly.

3. Remove from heat.

4. Mix in the almonds and cheddar cheese. Taste, and adjust the spices.

Vegan Option:

Omit the cheddar cheese and increase the corn to 3 cups. Saute finely diced onion in 1 tablespoon olive oil. Add the sauteed onion to the other ingredients in step 4. Salt to taste.

YIELD: 2 CUPS. FILLING FOR 4 ENCHILADAS

continues . . .

Green Pea Cream Cheese Enchilada Filling

This is an instant enchilada.

> 8 ounces cream cheese, at room temperature
> 2 cups fresh or frozen green peas

1. If you are using fresh green peas, steam them briefly, for about 1–2 minutes. Rinse in cold water to stop them cooking. Use frozen green peas just as they come from the package.

2. In a mixing bowl, knead the cream cheese with your hand until it is soft. Mix in the green peas with your hand.

YIELD: 2 CUPS. FILLING FOR 4 ENCHILADAS

Spinach Enchilada Filling

> 2 tablespoons olive oil
> 2 onions, diced
> 4 cloves of garlic, finely chopped
> 8–10 ounces fresh spinach, chopped (6 cups)
> ½ cup sliced black olives (optional)
> ½ teaspoon dried basil or 2 teaspoons finely chopped fresh basil
> ½ teaspoon black pepper
> ¼ teaspoon cayenne
> ½ cup grated cheddar or monterey jack cheese (*optional, non-vegan*)
> ½ cup sour cream

1. In a medium-size frying pan, heat the oil. Add the onion, garlic, and spinach, and saute until the spinach is completely wilted but still bright green. Mix in the black olives if desired, basil, pepper, and cayenne.

2. Turn off the heat, and mix in the cheese and sour cream. Taste and adjust the seasonings if needed.

Vegan Option:

Omit the cheese and use 16 ounces of fresh spinach. Be sure to add the sliced black olives. Salt to taste.

YIELD: 2 CUPS. FILLING FOR 4 ENCHILADAS

Pepper Olive Enchilada Filling

This filling has intense, exciting flavors. The method is important.

3 tablespoons olive oil

2 green peppers, diced in 1-inch squares

1 teaspoon coriander seeds

8 ounces cream cheese, at room temperature

½ cup coarsely chopped black olives

Freshly ground black pepper

¼ teaspoon cayenne

½ teaspoon ground coriander

1. Heat the oil in a medium-size frying pan. Add the green peppers and coriander seeds. Saute over high heat for about 5 minutes, stirring frequently, until the peppers are blistered, lightly browned, and fragrant. Remove from the heat.

2. Mix in the cream cheese, black olives, and spices.

YIELD: 2 CUPS. FILLING FOR 4 ENCHILADAS

Onion & Fresh Herb Enchilada Filling

2 onions, diced

¼ cup finely chopped fresh green herbs (I like parsley, chives, basil, dill, and fresh coriander leaves.)

½ cup sour cream

½ cup grated cheddar cheese

Freshly ground black pepper

Mix together all the ingredients.

YIELD: 2 CUPS. FILLING FOR 4 ENCHILADAS

continues . . .

Mushroom Enchilada Filling

    2 tablespoons olive oil

    10 ounces mushrooms, sliced (3–4 cups)

    1 onion, diced

    4 cloves of garlic, finely chopped

    ¼ teaspoon cayenne

    ½ teaspoon dried dill weed or 1 tablespoon finely chopped fresh dill

    ½ cup sour cream (*optional, non-vegan*)

1. Heat the oil in a medium-size frying pan. Add the mushrooms, onion, and garlic and saute for about 5 minutes, until the mushrooms are tender and most of the juice is cooked off. Mix in the cayenne and dill and cook for 1 minute more.

2. Turn off the heat and mix in the sour cream. Taste and adjust the seasonings.

Vegan Option: Omit sour cream, increase sliced mushrooms to 12–16 ounces. Salt to taste.

               YIELD: 2 CUPS. FILLING FOR 4 ENCHILADAS

Asparagus Enchilada Filling

    2 tablespoons olive oil

    3 cups asparagus cut in bite-size pieces

    2 cloves of garlic, finely chopped

    ¼ teaspoon dried or finely chopped fresh tarragon

    Freshly ground black pepper

    Juice of ½ lemon

    1 cup grated cheddar or monterey jack cheese (*optional, non-vegan*)

1. Heat the oil in a medium-size frying pan. Add the asparagus and saute until it is tender.

2. Add the garlic, tarragon, pepper, and lemon juice. Saute for 1 minute more.

3. Turn off the heat and mix in the cheese. Taste and adjust the seasonings.

Vegan Option: Omit cheese and use 4 cups asparagus. Salt to taste.

               YIELD: 2 CUPS. FILLING FOR 4 ENCHILADAS

Cabbagetown Enchilada Sauce

This enchilada sauce is a richly flavored and mildly spicy tomato-based sauce. I recommend it as a sauce for enchiladas, burritos, and chile rellenos.

    1 quart canned tomatoes or 6 fresh ripe tomatoes

    1 tablespoon ground cumin

    1 teaspoon ground coriander

    ½ teaspoon ground dried hot pepper

    ½ teaspoon dried or finely chopped fresh oregano

    ½ teaspoon dried basil or 2 teaspoons finely chopped fresh basil

    3 tablespoons light vegetable oil

    1 onion, finely chopped

    4 cloves of garlic, finely chopped

    ½ teaspoon salt

    2 green peppers, finely chopped

    ½ cup finely chopped fresh cilantro

1. Pour the tomatoes through a strainer or a colander mounted in a bowl to drain off some juice. You will need about 2 ½ cups of mostly drained tomatoes to make a thick salsa. (Save the juice to use in soup or in refried beans.)

2. Finely chop the drained tomatoes or squeeze them with your hands to make small pieces. If you are using fresh tomatoes, chop them up finely.

3. Measure out the spices and herbs and mix them together so they're ready to use.

4. In a medium-size frying pan, heat the oil. Add the onion and garlic and saute for 3–4 minutes, so they just start to cook. Reduce the heat and add the spice mixture. Saute for 1 minute to enhance the flavors, stirring constantly so nothing sticks and burns.

5. Add the tomatoes. Simmer canned tomatoes for 5 minutes, fresh tomatoes for 15 minutes. Add the salt and green peppers and simmer for 5 minutes more. Add the cilantro.

6. Taste and reseason. If you like hotter salsa, add more hot pepper.

YIELD: 3 CUPS

New Mexico Layered Red Chile Enchiladas

Since the Cabbagetown days I've lived many years in New Mexico, and have learned from great teachers to make the authentic New Mexico enchilada.

> 3 cups New Mexico Red Chile Sauce (page 107)
> Light vegetable oil for frying tortillas and sauteeing onions
> 2 small onions diced
> 12 corn tortillas
> 2 cups grated cheddar or monterey jack cheese or soft goat cheese,
>   OR 2 cups cooked pinto or anasazi beans (*vegan option*)

1. Prepare the Red Chile Sauce.

2. Heat about 2 tablespoons oil in a small frying pan. Fry each tortilla on one side, then turn over and cook until it is just starting to stiffen. Remove and drain on a paper towel or paper bag. Add more oil as necessary to fry all the tortillas.

3. Oil a medium-size casserole dish. Start layering enchiladas. The bottom layer is enough Red Chile Sauce to coat dish. Then add a layer of 4 tortillas, placed side by side. Use ½ of the onions in the next layer, sprinkle with ½ of the cheese or the beans. Then add more Red Chile Sauce. Then comes another layer of 4 tortillas, a layer of the remaining onions sprinkled with the remaining cheese or beans. Cover with more Red Chile Sauce. Top with the remaining 4 tortillas and a thick layer of Red Chile Sauce.

4. Bake in a preheated 350° oven for 30 minutes.

With Sauteed Onions, Green Peppers, & Corn

Saute the onions in 1 tablespoon oil until soft. Add ½ cup diced green peppers and ½ cup fresh corn kernels and saute until just cooked. Use as the onions layer in step 3.

YIELD: 4 SERVINGS

New Mexico Red Chile Sauce

This is a simple gravy, flavorful and fiery, based on large dried red chile peppers. You can cut the hotness by adding canned tomatoes, and can vary the taste by adding onions or cilantro. Red Chile Sauce is used frequently in Mexican cooking. Its companion, Green Chile Sauce, is such an art that I haven't mastered it yet. That will be in my next cookbook.

Large dried red chiles are commonly available in the Southwest, where they're called California, Anaheim, or New Mexico chiles. Different but similar varieties of chiles are called chile pasilla or chile ancho. The peppers are often strung in long braids called ristras. If you live on the East coast, you might be able to grow large hot peppers and dry them yourself, or you can find dried chiles in a good grocery store, or you can order them from Ranch O. Casados, my favorite supplier in New Mexico: PO Box 1149, San Juan Pueblo, NM, 87566.

6–8 large dried red chiles (about 4 ounces)

6 cloves garlic

3 cups boiling water

3 tablespoons butter OR olive oil (*vegan option*)

3 tablespoons whole wheat flour or cornmeal

1 teaspoon sea salt

1. Rinse the chiles, put them on a flat baking tray and roast them 8–12 minutes in a preheated 350° oven to bring the flavor to life. Be careful. They burn quickly. Every oven is different, so you'll want to check them frequently until you have a feeling for what's right for your oven and your peppers.

2. Pull off the chile stems. You may take out some of the seeds if you want a mild sauce since the seeds are the hottest part of the chile. I like leaving all the seeds in.

3. Puree the chiles, seeds and all, and the water with the garlic in a food processor or blender.

4. In a large saucepan, melt the butter or heat the olive oil. Whisk in the flour or cornmeal. Gradually whisk in the chile puree. Add the salt.

5. Bring the mixture up to a slow bubble, then simmer it 10 minutes or until it's thick, stirring occasionally. It should be saucy. If it's too thick, add more water.

6. Taste. Add more salt if needed.

continues . . .

Chile Sauce Variations

- If your sauce is too thick or is hotter than you like, after it's cooked (step 6), stir in up to 1 quart of coarsely mashed canned tomatoes. Taste again and adjust seasonings.

- Stir-fry 1 or 2 chopped onions in the butter or oil before you add the flour (step 4).

- Sprinkle finely minced fresh cilantro over the sauce just before it's finished cooking (end of step 5).

YIELD: 3 CUPS

Chile Rellenos

The chile relleno I like the best, after all our experiments, is basically a puffy omelet with a cheese-filled hot pepper in the center. The most commonly grown hot peppers in New York State are Cubanelles and Hungarian hot wax peppers. Whichever pepper you use, you want it to be about 4 inches long and at least 1 inch wide. After you make the puffy omelets, you bake them with salsa and cheese on top, and serve with rice and beans.

2 cups Refried Beans (page 2)

2 cups Herbed Brown Rice (page 69)

2 cups Cabbagetown Enchilada Sauce (page 105) or
    New Mexico Red Chile Sauce (page 107)

4 medium-size hot peppers

½ pound monterey jack or mild cheddar cheese

6 eggs, separated

4 tablespoons butter or cooking oil

1. First make the refried beans, rice, and sauce.

2. To prepare the hot peppers, broil them on a tray under the broiler of your oven, turning them once, until they're browned and blistery all over. Put them inside a paper bag and allow them to steam for 10 minutes. Cut off

the stems, pull off most of the thin outer skin, slit them about 2 inches down one side, and remove the seeds.

3. Slice part of the cheese into 4 finger-size pieces, and put 1 piece of cheese inside each hot pepper.

4. Beat the egg whites until stiff in a medium-size bowl. Beat the egg yolks until smooth in a separate bowl. Gradually fold the whites into the yolks, keeping the mixture as puffy as possible.

5. Melt 1 tablespoon of butter or heat the oil in a small frying pan or an omelet pan. Spoon some puffy egg batter about the size and shape of a stuffed hot pepper into the pan and allow it to cook for about 1 minute, until it is slightly firm. Lay a stuffed hot pepper gently in the batter, spoon some more batter over the top, and flip gently. Cook on the second side until this little puffy omelet is slightly golden around the edges and firm. Put on an individual ovenproof serving plate or on a buttered or oiled baking tray or dish, whichever you will use to bake the rellenos.

6. Melt more butter in the pan or add more oil and fry the remaining rellenos in a similar fashion. Keep stirring the eggs, since the yolks will separate out. Try to plan so you use all the batter.

7. Grate the remaining cheese.

8. If you are baking the rellenos on individual plates, cover each relleno with about ½ cup of sauce. Arrange ½ cup rice and ½ cup beans next to the relleno. Sprinkle it all with grated cheese. Or put all 4 rellenos in the baking dish, cover with sauce, and sprinkle with grated cheese. (Arrange hot rice and beans with rellenos on individual plates at serving time.)

9. Bake in a preheated 350° oven for 15–20 minutes, until the rellenos puff up and look luscious, and the cheese is melted and bubbly around the edge. Serve immediately.

YIELD: SERVES 4

Burritos

A burrito is a flour tortilla that is filled then rolled up. A standard filling is refried beans. The variation that follows is for a spicy scrambled egg filling. When you're buying flour tortillas, check the list of ingredients carefully. Many commercial flour tortillas are made with lard. Natural foods stores often carry flour tortillas made without lard and with whole wheat flour instead of white flour. The refried beans have to be hot when you make burritos, but other than that burritos require no cooking.

> 2 cups Refried Beans (page 2)
>
> 2 cups Cabbagetown Enchilada Sauce (page 105) or Salsa Fresca (page 4)
>
> 4 flour tortillas
>
> 2 cups grated monterey jack or cheddar cheese
>
> 2 cups finely shredded lettuce or spinach
>
> Sour cream or Guacamole (page 5)

1. First make the refried beans and sauce or salsa.

2. To assemble each burrito, sprinkle ½ cup grated cheese in a stripe down the center of a flour tortilla. Cover with a generous ½ cup of hot refried beans, and sprinkle with ½ cup of shredded lettuce or spinach. Roll the burrito up, and put it on serving plate with the seam side down.

3. Top each enchilada with ½ cup enchilada sauce or salsa fresca and a big dollop of sour cream or guacamole. Serve immediately.

Vegan Option:

Omit the cheese, sour cream, use vegan guacamole.

YIELD: SERVES 4

Breakfast Burritos

Instead of using refried beans, make up a scrambled egg filling.

 2 cups Cabbagetown Enchilada Sauce (page 105) or Salsa Fresca (page 4)
 4 flour tortillas
 8 eggs
 1 green pepper, finely diced
 ½ teaspoon ground cumin
 ¼ teaspoon cayenne
 2 tablespoons butter
 2 cups grated monterey jack or cheddar cheese
 2 cups finely shredded lettuce
 Sour cream or Guacamole

1. First make the sauce or salsa.

2. In a bowl, beat the eggs with green pepper, cumin, and cayenne.

3. Heat butter in a frying pan and cook the egg mixture in the butter until it is well scrambled.

4. Roll inside the flour tortillas with grated cheese and shredded lettuce. Top with Enchilada Sauce or Salsa Fresca and a big dollop of sour cream or Guacamole. Serve immediately.

YIELD: SERVES 4

Chick Pea Curry

This spicy chick pea and tomato dish has a classic spice combination.

> 2 cups uncooked chick peas
>
> 10 cups water
>
> 3–4 whole cloves
>
> 2–3 cardamom pods
>
> 1-inch piece stick cinnamon
>
> 10–12 black peppercorns
>
> 3 tablespoons light vegetable oil
>
> 2 whole cloves
>
> 1 cardamom pod
>
> 1-inch piece stick cinnamon
>
> 2 onions, finely chopped
>
> 4 cloves of garlic, finely chopped
>
> ½-inch piece fresh ginger, finely chopped
>
> 3 tomatoes, chopped
>
> 1 teaspoon salt
>
> 1 ½ teaspoons ground cumin
>
> ½ teaspoon ground coriander
>
> Chopped fresh cilantro (optional)

1. Sort the chick peas very carefully for stones and rinse. In a large pot combine the chick peas, water, 3–4 whole cloves, 2–3 cardamom pods, 1-inch piece stick cinnamon, and 10–12 peppercorns. Bring to a boil, then reduce the heat and simmer, partially covered, for 2–3 hours, until the chick peas are very tender. Pour through a colander to drain, and save the chick pea cooking liquid.

2. In a medium-size frying pan, heat the oil. Add the remaining cloves, cardamom pod, and cinnamon. Cook until the spices swell up, then add the onions. Saute until the onions are brown, then add the garlic and ginger. Saute for 2–3 minutes more. Add the tomatoes, and cook for about 10 minutes, until the tomatoes are soft.

3. Add the drained chick peas, salt, cumin, and coriander. Cook for 10–15 minutes, adding chick pea cooking liquid as needed to make a saucy consistency.

4. Serve garnished with chopped fresh cilantro leaves, if available.

YIELD: SERVES 6

Dry Potato Curry

This is very easy to prepare and makes a good all-purpose dish. Potatoes and Indian spices are meant for each other.

6 potatoes

¼ cup light vegetable oil

2 teaspoons black mustard seeds

½ teaspoon asafetida

1 teaspoon turmeric

3 onions, chopped

2 teaspoons ground cumin

2 teaspoons ground coriander

½ teaspoon cayenne

Juice of ½ lemon

1 teaspoon salt

1. Scrub the potatoes well but do not peel. Cook in water to cover until done but still firm, about 30 minutes after the water boils. Cut into bite-size pieces.

2. In a fairly large frying pan, heat the oil over medium heat. Add the mustard seeds and stir until they pop but do not burn. Add the asafetida and turmeric, then immediately add the onions. Stir until the onions are cooked.

3. Add the cumin, coriander, cayenne, and lemon juice. Then mix in the potatoes and salt, and cook for a few minutes.

4. Taste and serve immediately.

YIELD: SERVES 6

Cauliflower Curry

Another, different, vegetable curry. This dish is good eaten with plain rice or with parathas.

¼ cup light vegetable oil

2 teaspoons black mustard seeds

¼ teaspoon asafetida

1 teaspoon turmeric

½ cup dried unsweetened or grated fresh coconut

1 fresh hot pepper, finely chopped

4 cloves of garlic, finely chopped

½-inch piece fresh ginger, finely chopped

2 onions, chopped

1 quart canned tomatoes or 6–8 fresh ripe tomatoes, chopped

2 teaspoons salt

1 teaspoon molasses

1 tablespoon ground cumin

1 tablespoon ground coriander

1 head cauliflower, cut in bite-size pieces

1 cup water

2 green peppers, chopped, seeds and all

1. In a soup pot, heat the oil until a mustard seed dropped in it sizzles. Pour in the mustard seeds and cook until they pop. Lower the heat and stir frequently so you don't burn any of the seeds. Stir in the asafetida, then the turmeric, then the coconut. Add the chopped hot pepper, then the garlic and ginger and cook for about 5 minutes. Stir frequently so nothing sticks. If anything does start to stick, add more oil.

2. Add the onions. Stir and cook for 10 minutes. Crush the canned tomatoes by hand to get small pieces, or chop the fresh tomatoes. Add to the pot along with the salt, molasses, cumin, and the coriander.

3. Add the cauliflower and water. Cover and cook for 20 minutes, stirring occasionally.

4. Add the peppers. Cover and cook for 30 minutes, stirring occasionally.

5. Taste and adjust the seasonings.

Cauliflower Green Pea Curry

Add 2 cups fresh or frozen green peas about 15 minutes before you finish cooking.

Potato Green Pea Curry

Substitute 4 potatoes, cut in cubes, for the cauliflower. Add 2 cups green peas 15 minutes before you finish cooking.

YIELD: SERVES 6

Breakfast Bakery

My favorite breakfast has always been
and still is a good mug of dark-roast coffee with a delicious
whole-grain muffin or scone. Cinnamon buns and waffles are
for special occasions—perhaps a holiday brunch. Let their
aroma coming from the kitchen tempt your guests!

What else can you serve for breakfast? Besides fresh fruit or
fruit salad or juice (and coffee or tea), for something more
substantial you may want to try quiche or scrambled tofu. I
always like a big bowl of cooked steel-cut oats with banana.

The muffins, especially those with fruit, poppy seeds, or
nuts, and the scones are also suitable for coffee breaks and
tea time, lunch-box treats, or desserts.

Whole wheat pastry (not bread) flour is used in these
recipes. There's no sugar, either—
just honey or maple syrup.

82 Lemon Poppyseed Muffins

Crunchy, nicely textured vegan muffins.

 3 cups whole wheat pastry flour

 3 tablespoons baking powder

 2 teaspoons cinnamon

 ½ cup poppy seeds

 ½ pound tofu

 ¾ cup corn or canola oil

 ¾ cup maple syrup

 ¾ cup apple juice or water

 ¼ cup lemon juice

 2 teaspoons vanilla

 Grated zest (rind) of one lemon

1. In a large mixing bowl, mix together the dry ingredients: flour, baking powder, cinnamon, and poppy seeds.

2. Blend the tofu with other wet ingredients and lemon zest in a food processor or blender. If you are using a bowl, mash the tofu with a wooden spoon. Then, using a whisk, blend the tofu with the other wet ingredients and tofu as well as you can.

3. Mix the blended wet ingredients into dry ingredients mixture.

4. Spoon the batter into oiled muffin cups, filling them ⅔ full.

5. Bake in a preheated 350° oven for 25 minutes until the muffins are browning on top and firm.

YIELD: 18 MUFFINS

Vegan Corn Muffins

These are all delicious. Classic Vegan Corn Muffins are what it says—these plain corn muffins are great with fruit butters or preserves at breakfast or coffee break; or they could be served with soup. The addition of currants and walnuts in the second corn muffin recipe makes these muffins sweet and rich for your breakfast table. The third recipe, Vegan Corn Muffins with Fennel Seeds, is another classic corn muffin with a delicious touch of fennel. Using barley or oat flour in these muffins will give them an extra delicate texture.

Classic Vegan Corn Muffins

1 ½ cups cornmeal

1 ½ cups whole wheat pastry flour

1 tablespoon baking powder

½ teaspoon sea salt

½ cup corn oil

½ cup maple syrup

½ cup tofu

1 cup apple juice

1. In a medium-size mixing bowl, mix together the dry ingredients: cornmeal, whole wheat pastry flour, baking powder, and salt.

2. In a blender or food processor, blend the oil, maple syrup, tofu, and apple juice. If you are using a bowl, mash the tofu with a wooden spoon.
   Then, using a whisk, blend the tofu with the other wet ingredients as well as you can.

3. Mix the wet ingredients into the dry ones.

4. Oil muffin tins, and fill cups almost to the top.

5. Bake in a preheated 350° oven for 30 minutes or until an inserted knife comes out clean.

YIELD: 24 MUFFINS

Vegan Corn Muffins with Currants & Walnuts

½ cup dried currants

1 cup apple juice

1 ½ cups cornmeal

1 ½ cups whole wheat pastry flour

1 tablespoon baking powder

½ teaspoon sea salt

1 teaspoon cinnamon

1 cup chopped walnuts

½ cup corn oil

½ cup maple syrup

1 teaspoon vanilla

½ cup tofu

1. Combine currants and apple juice in a saucepan and bring to a slow boil. Turn down heat and let simmer for 1 or 2 minutes. Drain the currants reserving the apple juice for later in the recipe. Set both aside to cool.

2. In a medium-size mixing bowl, mix together the dry ingredients: cornmeal, whole wheat pastry flour, baking powder, salt, and cinnamon.

3. Toss the nuts and currants into the dry mixture, mixing well.

4. In a blender or food processor, blend the oil, maple syrup, vanilla, tofu, and apple juice. If you are using a bowl, mash the tofu with a wooden spoon. Then, using a whisk, blend the tofu with the other wet ingredients and tofu as well as you can.

5. Mix the wet ingredients into the dry ones.

6. Oil muffin tins, and fill cups to the top.

7. Bake in a preheated 350° oven for 30 minutes or until an inserted knife comes out clean.

YIELD: 24 MUFFINS

continues . . .

Vegan Corn Muffins with Fennel Seeds

2 cups whole wheat pastry flour or 1 cup barley flour plus 1 cup whole
   wheat pastry flour or 1 cup oat flour plus 1 cup whole wheat pastry flour

2 cups cornmeal

1 tablespoon fennel seeds

1 ½ tablespoons baking powder

½ teaspoon sea salt

2 cups water

½ cup maple syrup

½ cup corn oil

1. If possible, grind fresh barley or oat flour.

2. Mix the flour, cornmeal, fennel seeds, baking powder, and salt in a large mixing bowl.

3. Make a well in the center of the dry ingredients. In it mix together the water, maple syrup, and corn oil.

4. Mix the wet ingredients in with the dry ones.

5. Let the batter sit for ½ hour before pouring into the muffin cups. (This recipe produces a delicate crumb texture, and this step helps the baked muffins to hold together.)

6. Oil muffin tins, and fill cups with batter to the top.

7. Bake in a preheated 350° oven for 30 minutes or until an inserted knife comes out clean. Let the muffins cool in the pan for a few minutes before you remove them or they will fall apart.

YIELD: 24 MUFFINS

Sunday Brunch Muffins

This is a classic Cabbagetown recipe. You can make a muffin mix the night before. Mix together the dry ingredients in one bowl or covered refrigerator container and the wet ingredients in another. Store in the refrigerator overnight, mix them together in the morning, and bake.

2 cups whole wheat pastry flour

1 tablespoon baking powder

¼ teaspoon salt

2 teaspoons cinnamon

¼ teaspoon nutmeg or ground cardamom

½ teaspoon allspice or powdered ginger

½ cup raisins or chopped dates

½ cup walnuts or almonds, coarsely chopped

Grated rind of 2 oranges

1 cup chopped fresh fruit
   (apples, pears, peaches, bananas, blueberries, or cranberries)

2 eggs

½ cup honey

1 cup milk

1 teaspoon vanilla or almond extract

½ cup butter, melted

1. In a medium-size mixing bowl, mix together all the dry ingredients: flour, baking powder, salt, and spices. Add the dried fruit and nuts, the orange rind, and the chopped fresh fruit or berries.

2. In a separate bowl, mix the eggs, honey, milk, vanilla, and butter.

3. Make a well in the center of the dry ingredients. Pour in the wet ingredients, and mix together until well blended.

4. Butter a muffin tin well—the bottoms and sides of the cups, and the area on the top between muffin cups. Fill each muffin cup as full as you can get it with batter. You will have enough batter for 9–12 muffins. Put the muffin tin on a flat baking tray in case any of the batter spills over.

continues . . .

5. Bake in a preheated 350° oven for about 40 minutes, or until the muffins are evenly browned and firm. Let sit for about 5 minutes to firm up before removing the muffins from the pan.

Coconut Muffins

Substitute 1 cup dried or grated fresh coconut for the nuts in the recipe.

Oatmeal Muffins

Add ½ cup of rolled oats to the batter after it is all mixed. This will make heartier, chewier muffins.

Poppyseed Muffins

Mix ½ cup of poppy seeds with the milk in a small pot. Simmer over medium heat for about 5 minutes, then add to the wet ingredients as you would plain milk. The poppy seeds give the muffins a nice crunch.

YIELD: 9–12 MUFFINS

Cinnamon Buns

Making these is an ambitious undertaking but worth it as you uncurl them and the raisins and walnuts spill out.

Dough (steps 1–5)
2 cups milk
½ cup butter
¾ cup honey
Grated rind of 1 lemon
1 tablespoon active dry yeast
2 eggs, lightly beaten
3–4 cups whole wheat bread flour

Filling (step 6)

½ cup butter, at room temperature

1 cup honey

Grated rind of 2 oranges

2 teaspoons cinnamon

1 cup walnuts, coarsely chopped

1 cup raisins

1. In a small pot, heat the milk and butter until the butter is melted.

2. Measure the honey and lemon rind into a bread bowl. Pour in the hot milk-butter mixture and stir until the honey is dissolved. While it's still warm, drop in the yeast. Leave the milk-yeast mixture for about 5 minutes, while the yeast dissolves and begins to foam.

3. Stir in the eggs, then about 3 cups of flour, enough to make a loose dough.

4. Allow to rise in a warm spot for 1 hour.

5. Turn the dough onto a floured counter, and knead in additional flour only until the dough holds together in a ball. You want the dough to be a little gooey and difficult to work with so your pastries will be lighter. Flour the counter well, and using a rolling pin, roll out the dough into the largest rectangle you can make, about 12 inches by 24 inches.

6. Cream together the butter, honey, orange rind, and cinnamon for the filling. Spread evenly over the dough. Sprinkle on the walnuts and the raisins.

7. Roll up the dough into a long cylinder. Cut it into slices each about 1 inch thick—18–24 slices. Place slices in a well buttered 9-inch by 13-inch baking dish, or 2 or 3 pie plates.

8. Allow to rise in a warm spot for 1 hour until more than double.

9. Bake in preheated 350° oven for 30–40 minutes, until the buns are evenly browned.

YIELD: 18-24 BUNS

86 Grandma's Norwegian Oatmeal Waffles

Back in the good old days, my grandmother and grandfather ran a Norwegian waffle house in Brooklyn. There were lines around the block waiting to get in. One Christmas my grandparents wanted to go to a big party the relatives were throwing, so they sold the restaurant. I like that story. The oatmeal gives the waffles an extra chewiness.

    2 cups milk
    2 cups rolled oats
    2 eggs, separated
    ⅓ cup butter, melted
    ⅓ cup whole wheat pastry flour
    1 tablespoon baking powder
    ¼ teaspoon salt

1. Heat the milk until scalded, then pour it over the rolled oats in a medium-size bowl. Cool for about 30 minutes.

2. Mix in the egg yolks, melted butter, flour, baking powder, and salt.

3. Beat the egg whites until stiff, and fold into the batter.

4. Make the waffles following the directions for your waffle iron. Butter the waffle iron thoroughly, since these waffles are very tender and have a tendency to stick.

5. Serve warm. The traditional accompaniments are butter and homemade jams; butter and maple syrup; and yogurt, maple syrup, and fresh fruit.

Grandma's Oatmeal Pancakes

Make the batter exactly as for waffles. Fry the pancakes in butter in a large frying pan, flipping once.

YIELD: 4 WAFFLES OR 12 PANCAKES.

SERVES 4

Mindy's Scones

One of my first jobs in the food business was working as a waitress in a teahouse in England. The staff used to jump on the chance to get the fresh scones as they were brought from the bakery every morning. And for the British, as with everyone else, scones are also wonderful at tea time. This scone recipe is from my friend Mindy.

> **2 cups whole wheat pastry flour**
>
> **2 cups unbleached organic white flour**
>
> **1½ tablespoons plus 1 teaspoon baking powder**
>
> **½ teaspoon baking soda**
>
> **1 cup dried currants**
>
> **½ pound butter, cubed**
>
> **2 tablespoons grated lemon or orange rind (optional)**
>
> **¼ cup honey**
>
> **1½ cups heavy cream (You can substitute yoghurt, buttermilk, or nonfat buttermilk for the cream.)**
>
> **1 egg, beaten with fork (optional: to glaze the scones before baking)**

1. Mix the dry ingredients together: flour, baking powder, and baking soda. (Do not use all whole wheat pastry flour or the scones will crumble apart. The white flour makes scones flakier and rise slightly higher.)

2. Add the currants.

3. Slowly add the butter. Cut in with 2 forks until it is cut in tiny pieces.

4. Add the grated lemon or orange rind and the honey.

5. Add heavy cream mixing only until the dough comes together.

6. Form the dough into 2 logs and chill until ready to use (give it at least a half hour to rest).

7. Divide each log into 2 pieces (you'll have 4 pieces altogether). Roll out each piece on a floured surface into a circular shape approximately 8 inches in diameter. You want the rolled-out dough to be ½ inch thick so it will rise into a nice puffy scone.

continues . . .

8. Cut each circle into 6 triangles. Each triangle is 1 scone (24 scones in all).

9. Lay the scones on a large buttered baking tray. Leave room between the scones as they will rise.

10. Glaze the tops of the scones with egg, if desired, for a golden crusty top.

11. Bake in a preheated 350° oven for 20 minutes until golden.

YIELD: 24 SCONES

Desserts

"Everything good in moderation"—
this is my philosophy on desserts. The recipes in this selection
are the best of the best. For the most part they are simple to
make and include cakes, pies, crisps, cobblers, and cookies.
Many of the fruit recipes can be varied with different fruits. For
example, Stina's Apple Cake is wonderful with fresh summer
peaches as a variation. Many of these cakes, cobblers, and crisps,
especially when warm, go well with ice cream or whipped
cream, or non-dairy ice cream.

All of the recipes in this chapter are made with natural
sweeteners, honey or maple syrup. They use whole wheat pastry
flour (not bread flour). They're nutritionally rich and it's
astounding how delicious they all are.

If you don't have a baking pan of the size and type
recommended in recipe, substitute the closest sized pan you
have. Remember that most desserts expand when baking, so
when you're filling a pan, don't push your luck and overfill it.
Just bake an extra little pie or cake.

So be happy—conclude a healthy friendly meal
with something sweet and yummy!

Carrot Cake

This exceptionally rich, delicious, easy-to-make cake is consistently good.

1 cup honey OR maple syrup (*vegan option*)

1 cup grated raw carrot

1 cup raisins, or combination raisins and chopped dates

1 teaspoon cinnamon

1 teaspoon nutmeg

½ teaspoon cloves

½ cup butter OR corn oil or canola oil (*vegan option*)

1 cup water

2 cups whole wheat pastry flour

2 teaspoons baking soda

¾ cup coarsely chopped walnuts or hazelnuts

1. In a medium-size pot combine the honey or maple syrup, carrot, raisins, spices, butter or oil, and water. Bring to a boil and boil for 5 minutes, stirring frequently. Remove from the heat and allow to cool to lukewarm, about 45 minutes.

2. Measure the flour into a mixing bowl. Rub the baking soda between your hands to remove any lumps, and mix into the flour along with the nuts.

3. Make a well in the center of the flour mixture and pour in the cooled carrot mixture. Mix the dry and wet ingredients together thoroughly.

4. Pour into a well-buttered or well-oiled (vegan) 10-inch springform pan or any equivalent-size pan or pans.

5. Bake in a preheated 325° oven for 40 minutes, or until the cake is lightly browned, firm, and a knife inserted in the center comes out clean.

6. Allow to cool for 15 minutes before removing from the pan.

YIELD: ONE 10-INCH CAKE.

SERVES 8

Johnny Appleseed Cake

This is the cake my mother made me every birthday and so it has a special place in my heart.

1 ½ cups applesauce or 3–4 apples, cored and diced

2 cups whole wheat pastry flour

1 teaspoon cinnamon

½ teaspoon nutmeg

¼ teaspoon cloves

1 cup raisins

1 cup coarsely chopped walnuts

½ cup butter OR corn oil OR canola oil *(vegan option)*

⅔ cup honey OR maple syrup *(vegan option)*

2 teaspoons baking soda

1. If you are using fresh apples, put them in a medium-size pot with 2 tablespoons of water. Simmer covered for about 30 minutes, or until the apples have become hot, thick applesauce. Measure out 1½ cups and return to the pot to keep it warm. If you are using applesauce, put it in a saucepan and warm it over low heat.

2. Mix together the flour, spices, raisins, and walnuts in a mixing bowl.

3. Melt the butter in a small pot. Mix in the honey or maple syrup. If you are using corn or canola oil, mix with the honey or maple syrup in a small bowl. Stir into the dry ingredients.

4. Stir the baking soda into the hot applesauce in the pot. This will foam up in a spectacular fashion—partly responsible for my love of this cake. Add to the batter in the bowl and mix thoroughly.

5. Pour the batter into a well-buttered or well-oiled (vegan) 9-inch square cake pan.

6. Bake in a preheated 325° oven for about 40 minutes, or until a knife inserted in the center comes out clean.

7. Serve warm or cool.

YIELD: ONE 9-INCH SQUARE CAKE.

SERVES 8

Stina's Apple Cake

This is the most famous recipe in *Wings of Life*. It's a good one for creative fruit uses—try substituting 1 cup sliced peaches, plums, nectarines, apricots, or pears for the apples.

> 2 big apples
>
> 2 teaspoons cinnamon
>
> 2 cups whole wheat pastry flour
>
> 1 teaspoon baking soda
>
> ½ cup butter
>
> I cup honey
>
> ½ cup buttermilk or ½ cup whole milk soured with 1 teaspoon
>   of lemon juice
>
> 2 teaspoons pure vanilla extract

1. Core and slice the apples and mix them with the cinnamon. Set aside.

2. Mix the flour and baking soda. Using 2 forks or a pastry blender, cut the butter into the flour until the butter is in small pieces and evenly mixed.

3. Make a well in the center of the flour and butter, and in the well mix the honey, buttermilk or milk-and-lemon-juice mixture, and vanilla. Mix them into the flour and butter, stirring just enough to combine.

4. Butter a 9-inch cast iron frying pan, or a 9-inch round deep cake pan. Put in some batter, then a layer of apples, then batter. Continue layering until everything is used up. End with batter on top. (Fill the pan only O full. If you have extra batter and apples, bake them in another pan.)

5. Bake in a preheated 350° oven for 35 to 40 minutes, or until the center of the cake is firm.

YIELD: 9-INCH ROUND CAKE.

SERVES 8

Rhubarb Custard Pie

This is an exceptionally good rhubarb pie recipe. It's the first fruit pie I make each year.

> 9-inch or 10-inch Whole Wheat Pie Crusts (page 87)
> 4 cups chopped rhubarb
> ¾ cup honey
> 3 tablespoons whole wheat pastry flour
> ¼ teaspoon nutmeg
> Juice of 1 orange
> 1 egg
> 2 tablespoons butter

1. Follow the pie crust recipe to make dough for 9- or 10-inch bottom and top crusts. Roll out half the pie dough for your bottom crust, and fit it into a well-buttered 9-inch or 10-inch pie pan. Roll out the other half of the dough as a flat round about 2 inches wider than the top of the pie pan. Set aside.

2. Mix together the rhubarb, honey, flour, nutmeg, orange juice, and egg in a mixing bowl.

3. Pour the filling into the prepared pie shell. If it seems too full pour extra filling into a small buttered dish and bake when you bake the pie. Dot the filling with butter.

4. To make a lattice top, cut the flat round of pie crust into 8 strips about ¾ inch wide. Lay 4 of them parallel across the top of the pie. Then weave the other 4 pieces, 1 at a time, through the base pieces. Start them alternately on the top and on the bottom, so you have a real weaving. Pinch the edges of the lattice together with the bottom crust. Then merge them by fluting the rim of the crust.

5. Bake in a preheated 350° oven for about 50 minutes, or until the lattice crust is lightly browned and the filling is bubbly.

Strawberry Rhubarb Custard Pie

Substitute 2 cups sliced fresh strawberries for 2 cups of rhubarb. Decrease the honey to ½ cup.

YIELD: ONE 9-INCH OR 10-INCH PIE.

SERVES 6–8

Apple Pie

Classic and delicious. Really, what could be better than apple pie? Not much!

> 9-inch or 10-inch Whole Wheat Pie Crusts (page 87)
>
> 6 cups sliced apples (We leave the skins on when we slice the apples.)
>
> Juice of ½ lemon
>
> ¼ cup honey OR maple syrup (*vegan option*)
>
> ¼ cup whole wheat pastry flour
>
> ½ teaspoon cinnamon
>
> 2 tablespoons butter (See note in step 3.)

1. Follow the pie crust recipe to make dough for 9-inch or 10-inch bottom and top crusts. Roll out half the dough for your bottom crust, and fit it into a well-buttered 9-inch or 10-inch pie pan. Roll out the other half of the dough as a flat round about 2 inches wider than the top of the pie pan. Set aside.

2. Mix together the sliced apples, lemon juice, honey or maple syrup, pastry flour, and cinnamon in a mixing bowl.

3. Pour the filling into the pie shell. If there seems to be too much filling, pour extra filling into a small buttered or oiled dish and bake when you bake the pie. Dot the filling with butter unless you're making a vegan pie.

4. Place the top crust over the pie, press the rims together, turn them under, and flute for decoration. Slash the top of the pie with an A or with a design to let the steam escape.

5. Bake in a preheated 350° oven for 45–50 minutes, until the crust is golden brown and the filling looks delicious and bubbly.

6. Serve warm, plain, or with vanilla or lemon cinnamon ice cream, or with cheddar cheese.

Apple Cranberry Pie

Use 2 cups cranberries and 4 cups sliced apples. Increase the honey to ⅓ cup.

Fresh Fruit Pie

Instead of apples use cherries, blueberries, peaches, pears, plums, or any combination of fruits you like.

Vegan Option:

Make the Vegan Whole Wheat Pie Crusts on page 88. Oil any dishes for baking extra filling. Serve plain.

YIELD: ONE 9-INCH OR 10-INCH PIE.

SERVES 6-8

Date Nut Bars

These bars are chewy and sweet.

¼ cup butter
½ cup maple syrup
2 eggs, lightly beaten
2 cups coarsely chopped dates
1 cup coarsely chopped walnuts
½ cup plus 1 tablespoon whole wheat pastry flour
½ teaspoon baking powder

1. In a medium-size pot, melt the butter. Remove from the heat. Mix in the maple syrup, and as soon as the mixture has cooled a little, mix in the eggs. Add the dates and walnuts.

2. Combine the flour and baking powder and add to the mixture in the pot.

3. Pour the batter into a well-buttered 9-inch square baking pan. Bake in a preheated 350° oven for 45–50 minutes, or until the center is firm.

4. When cool, cut into bars.

YIELD: 24 BARS

Apple Crisp

You can make a crisp with any fruit or fruit combination that's in season, or you can use frozen fruits in the winter. Gobble it up warm for a very satisfying completion to a meal.

Fruit (step 1)

    8 cups sliced apples

    Juice of 1 lemon

    1 teaspoon cinnamon

    ½ teaspoon nutmeg

    ½ cup honey, OR maple syrup (*vegan option*)

Topping (step 2)

    3 cups rolled oats

    2 cups whole wheat pastry flour

    ½ teaspoon baking powder

    1 cup cold butter, grated, OR

        1 cup corn or canola oil (*vegan option*)

    ½ cup honey, OR maple syrup (*vegan option*)

    ½ teaspoon vanilla extract

    1–2 cups chopped toasted walnuts (optional)

1. Mix together the fruit ingredients to make the filling. Pat the mixture into a well-buttered or well-oiled (vegan) 9-inch by 13-inch baking dish.

2. In a medium-size bowl, mix together the topping ingredients with your fingers. Crumble the topping over the fruit mixture.

3. Bake in a preheated 350° oven for 45–60 minutes, until the crisp topping is evenly golden brown. Since some ovens bake unevenly, it's a good idea to check the crisp and turn the pan around after 30 minutes.

4. Serve while still warm if possible. Fruit crisps are great alone, but even more sumptuous with vanilla ice cream on top.

Apple Rhubarb Crisp

Use 4 cups sliced apples and 4 cups chopped rhubarb in the filling. Increase the honey or maple syrup to ¾ cup.

Apple Strawberry Crisp

Use 4 cups sliced strawberries and 4 cups sliced apples.

Black Raspberry, Red Raspberry, or Blackberry Crisp

Use 8 cups of berries in the filling.

Cherry Crisp

Use 8 cups sweet or sour pitted cherries. For the sour cherries increase the honey or maple syrup to ¾ cup.

Peach Crisp

Use 8 cups sliced peaches.

Blueberry Crisp

Use 8 cups blueberries.

Pear Crisp

Use 8 cups sliced pears.

Apple Cranberry Crisp

Use 4 cups sliced apples and 4 cups cranberries in the filling. Increase the honey or maple syrup to ¾ cup.

Vegan Option:

Serve with non-dairy ice cream.

YIELD: ONE 9-INCH BY 13-INCH PAN.

SERVES 8

Very Berry Cobbler

Guest feedback forms from Omega rated this dessert "Killer." The batter for this topping is liquidy, but it firms up as it bakes. The textures are part of the magic and charm of this juicy cobbler.

Filling (step 1)

3 cups berries, fresh or frozen, alone or in combination
  (large strawberries should be sliced)
1 tablespoon arrowroot powder
¼–½ cup water (For juicer berries, use the smaller amount of water.)
½ cup maple syrup
½ teaspoon grated lemon rind
4 teaspoons lemon juice
2 teaspoons corn oil
½ teaspoon sea salt

Topping (steps 2–3)

1 cup whole wheat pastry flour
½ teaspoon sea salt
½ teaspoon baking powder
¼ cup water
½ cup maple syrup
½ teaspoon vanilla extract
¼ cup corn oil

1. Dissolve the arrowroot powder in the water, then mix in the remaining filling ingredients ending with the fruit. Pour the filling into an oiled 9-inch by 13-inch baking dish.

2. Combine the dry ingredients (flour, salt, and baking powder) for the topping in a mixing bowl. Make a well in the center of the dry mixture and stir together the topping's liquid ingredients (water, maple syrup, vanilla, and oil). Stir the liquid mixture into the dry.

3. Pour the topping batter over the filling.

4. Bake in a preheated 350° oven for 40 minutes.

YIELD: ONE 9-INCH BY 13-INCH BAKING PAN.

SERVES 8

Blueberry Cobbler

This simple cobbler recipe is a good way to serve any juicy fruit or berry. Plan to make it shortly before you want to serve it, so the cobbler is still warm.

Fruit (steps 1–2)

4 cups blueberries

Juice of ½ lemon

½ teaspoon cinnamon

¼ cup honey

3 tablespoons cold butter, grated

Topping (steps 3–4)

5 tablespoons butter

½ cup honey

1 egg

1 cup whole wheat pastry flour

1 ½ teaspoons baking powder

¼ teaspoon cinnamon

¼ cup milk

1. Mix together the blueberries, lemon juice, cinnamon, honey, and butter.

2. Pour mixture into a well-buttered 9-inch square pan or a 10-inch round pan.

3. To make the topping, cream 5 tablespoons butter with ½ cup honey. Beat in the egg. Mix together the dry ingredients. Add to the creamed mixture alternately with the milk.

4. Spread the topping as smoothly as possible over the fruit.

5. Bake in a preheated 325° oven for 40–45 minutes, until the cobbler is lightly browned and a knife inserted in the center comes out clean. Do not overbake or the cobbler will be tough.

6. Serve plain or with vanilla ice cream.

Fresh Fruit Cobbler

Use 4 cups any fruit or fruit combination—berries, cherries, sliced peaches or pears (for example, 2 cups chopped rhubarb plus 2 cups sliced strawberries) in the filling.

YIELD: ONE 9-INCH SQUARE OR 10-INCH ROUND PAN.

SERVES 6

Carob Brownies

You can truly love these and not even think of chocolate.

1 cup butter

1 cup carob

⅔ cup honey

4 eggs, separated

1 teaspoon vanilla extract

1 cup chopped almonds or walnuts

⅓ cup whole wheat pastry flour

1 teaspoon baking powder

1. Melt the butter in a medium-size pot. Remove from the heat. Stir in the carob. Then mix in the honey, egg yolks, vanilla, and nuts.

2. Mix together the flour and baking powder and stir into the wet ingredients.

3. Beat the egg whites until stiff. Fold into the batter.

4. Pour into a well-buttered 9-inch square pan.

5. Bake in a preheated 350° oven for about 40 minutes, or until the brownies are firm.

6. Serve immediately while still warm, or cool in the pan before cutting and serving.

YIELD: 9 BROWNIES

Maple Lace Cookies

I received more letters about this cookie than about any other recipe in *Wings of Life*. Whether the cookies lace out or not depends on exactly what kind of flour and what kind of rolled oats you are using. If you make these cookies once and they don't spread out, make them with less flour the next time. Lace cookies have a very fragile texture so remember to handle them carefully.

½ cup butter

2 cups rolled oats

¾ cup maple syrup

1 teaspoon vanilla extract

¼ teaspoon salt

1 teaspoon baking soda

1½ cups whole wheat pastry flour

1. In a medium-size bowl, beat the butter until smooth. Beat in the oats, then the maple syrup, then the vanilla.

2. Stir in the salt, then the baking soda, then the flour. Stir until smooth.

3. Drop the batter by teaspoonfuls onto a buttered cookie sheet. Leave the cookies room to spread out. Bake in a preheated 325° oven for about 15 minutes or until the cookies are firm. Let the cookies cool for a few minutes on the baking sheets before you carefully remove them, as they are very fragile.

YIELD: 36 COOKIES

Peanut Butter Oatmeal Cookies

A good all purpose cookie. Kids of all ages love them.

½ cup butter OR corn oil or canola oil (*vegan option*)

1 cup peanut butter

½ cup honey OR maple syrup (*vegan option*)

1 egg (*optional, non-vegan*)

1 teaspoon vanilla extract

1 ½ cups whole wheat pastry flour

½ cup rolled oats

½ teaspoon baking soda

1 cup carob chips or 1 cup "non-natural chocolate chips sweetened with white sugar"

1. Beat the butter or oil and peanut butter until creamy. Add the honey or maple syrup and stir thoroughly. Mix in the egg, if you are using it, and vanilla. Stir well.

2. Combine the dry ingredients (flour, oats, and baking soda). Stir into the wet ingredients until well-mixed.

3. Fold in the chips.

4. Drop the batter by teaspoonfuls onto a buttered or oiled (vegan) cookie sheet. Make big cookies using tablespoonfuls of batter. Bake in a preheated 350° for about 20–25 minutes, until lightly browned.

Walnut & Raisin Cookies

All obvious good and wonderful things can be added to the recipe, especially raisins and walnuts.

YIELD: 18–24 COOKIES

Maple Almond Thumbprint Cookies

Awesome! No other word can describe this classic yet simple cookie, perfect for special and everyday occasions.

3 cups almonds, finely chopped

4 cups whole wheat pastry flour or barley flour

1 teaspoon cinnamon

¼ teaspoon salt

1 cup maple syrup

1 cup corn oil or canola oil

½ cup raspberry jam or apple butter

1. Finely chop almonds or pulse in a food processor.

2. Mix together all the ingredients except for the jam in a mixing bowl.

3. Using a heaping tablespoon, drop batter on an oiled cookie sheet, 2 inches apart.

4. Make a thumbprint in the middle of each cookie.

5. Fill each thumbprint with jam or apple butter.

6. Bake in a preheated 350° oven for 18–20 minutes or until golden.

YIELD: ABOUT 36 COOKIES

Index